RURAL LIFE IN THE
VALE OF THE WHITE HORSE

Rural Life in the Vale of the White Horse 1780-1914

A Berkshire Book

by

Nigel Hammond

William Smith (Booksellers) Ltd
35-41 London Street
Reading Berkshire

By the same author
THE WHITE HORSE COUNTRY (1972)

Contents

KEY TO REFERENCE ABBREVIATIONS

BAJ	Berkshire Archaeological Journal
BB	Bygone Berkshire, P. H. Ditchfield
BD	Billing's Directory, 1854
DDU	Digest of Directories — Uffington
DNB	Dictionary of National Biography
JOJ	Jackson's Oxford Journal
MacDermot	History of the G.W.R.
Mavor	A General Survey of the Agriculture of Berkshire, William Mavor, 1809
PD	Pigot's Directory, 1823
WHC	The White Horse Country

Illustrations

THE PHOTOGRAPHS

Acknowledgements and thanks for permission to reproduce photographs are due to The Museum of English Rural Life, University of Reading, for plates 9, 11, 16, 17, 18 and 30; to *The Oxford Mail & Times* for plate 32; *The London Illustrated News* for plate 63; Miss D. M. Booker for plates 26 and 67, Abingdon School Archives for plates 58, 59 and 68 and Cambridge University Library for plate 54.

MAPS

A DESCRIPTION OF FARMING IN THE
VALE OF THE WHITE HORSE ABOUT 1813

Along the Oxford Heights the country is very good dry corn land, though in parts too sandy. Gently descending to the south is the fertile Vale of Berkshire which crosses the country from Shrivenham to Cholsey. At present the western part of this Vale is employed as pasture land, chiefly dairy, while the sides and eastern part may be reckoned some of the most productive wheat land in the kingdom.

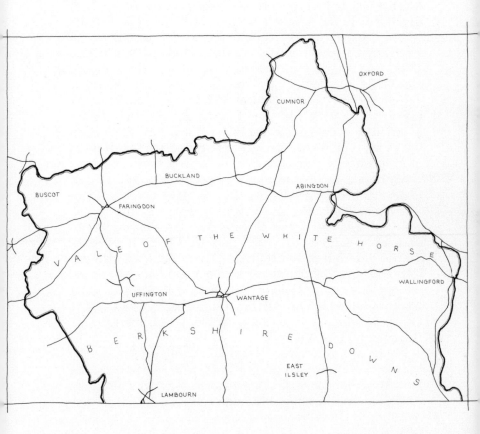

Note by the Author

Rural Life in the Vale of the White Horse complements my previous book, *The White Horse Country*, in which I made an historical survey of the scattered towns and villages in Berkshire's Vale of the White Horse. In this present book I deal with the same broad region of southern England between about 1780 and 1914, covering principally the social, economic, political, agricultural and industrial activities of four towns, Abingdon, Faringdon, Wallingford and Wantage, and numerous rural settlements lying scattered between them. I have included reference to such centres as Oxford, Reading, Swindon, Newbury, Bristol and London, where their importance influences the economy of the White Horse Vale. I have also used the time bracket 1780-1914 only as a broad indication of period; for in agriculture I have traced some developments from before 1780, and other topics I have taken to their logical conclusion beyond 1914, for instance, the Wantage Tramway. This study in local history also considers the previous economic and social geography of the region; additionally it contains a wealth of information about rural life which should have a ready application to other regions of England.

My thanks are due to countless people who have helped make this book possible; not least to Mr. Peter Bradley of *The North Berks Herald* series of newspapers, and to the editor of *Thames Valley Countryside*, for allowing me to draw upon material originally published in their journals. To the librarian of the House of Lords for help with the *Wantage Act, 1828*, to the British Museum, the librarians of the Berkshire County Libraries at Wantage and Abingdon, the Oxford City Library, the Berkshire Records Office, Reading, and to that most helpful of libraries, the Bodleian Library, Oxford.

I have also drawn upon material made available by the Museum of English Rural Life at Reading University, the Folk Museum, Gloucester, and to a lesser extent material in Abingdon and Newbury Museums.

I am grateful to Mrs. Bramley of Wantage for completing so much of the typing, to Andrew Smith of Abingdon School for his skilfully drawn maps and to Mr. H. T. Randolph for reading the manuscript and proofs with such meticulous care, but final responsibility for the book's content rests entirely with myself.

Abingdon   N.K.H.

Introduction

The Vale of the White Horse and the Berkshire Downs are probably one of Britain's best examples of a chalk ridge and clay vale structure. The Vale extends from the Ridgeway for some ten miles to the upper Thames, a countryside reminiscent of mutton, milk and serenity, where rolling downland and isolated beech woods form a characteristic landscape, giving way in the depth of the Vale to flat fields, elm-encompassed lanes and willow-fringed brooks. Towards the northern edge the Vale begins to rise up the back of the Corallian Limestone scarp from which the land drops away affording splendid panoramas over the upper-Thames valley.

Scenery, tree growth, brook and river patterns, direction of the routeways, the extent and scope of agricultural activity, are all in the broadest sense related to geology and soil deposits. Should one take a transect from the Thames at Newbridge (Kingston Bagpuize) to the chalk summit at Sparsholt Firs, one crosses the six geological divisions of the Vale, whose outcrops run from east to west along the Vale of the White Horse.

At Newbridge one finds a distinctly confined valley in which the Thames meanders over alluvium above Oxford Clay. Clay and alluvium produce lush water-meadows bordered by a profusion of elm and willow trees. Dairy farming is common from the outskirts of north Oxford along the river to Buscot on the Gloucestershire border.

Very gently the Oxford Clay dips southwards under the geologically younger structure of the Corallian Limestone which presents that distinctively sharp scarp-slope overlooking the river valley. A string of largely limestone-built villages stretch along the dip slope just below the crest; such places as Kingston Bagpuize, Hinton Waldrist, Buckland, Coleshill and Cumnor characterize the more important settlements. Giving light and warm soils, the area supports considerable acreages of wheat and barley in places where it is not devoted to market gardening, soft-fruit cultivation, hops and orchards.

1

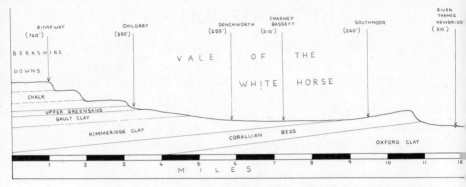

In turn the Corallian Limestone is overlaid to its south by a band of Kimmeridge Clay — a distinctively coloured deep blue-black area — taking its name from outcrops of the same structure on the Dorset coast. In the Vale this clay forms a stiff cold soil extending in a discontinuous zone along the river Ock from Abingdon to Longcot with everywhere abundant elm and willow trees, and some oak and ash. It is at present predominantly a zone of mixed arable and pasture farms, but before suitable ploughs could till the soil, and sufficiently sophisticated methods were developed to drain it, this was almost exclusively a pastoral area. Hereabouts, in the depth of the Vale, the closely nucleated villages were once islands surrounded by forest and marshland. As a place-name ending -*ey* means island, and we have Hanney — island frequented by wild cocks, Goosey — Goose island, Charney Bassett — island on the river Churn (or Ock), Pusey — Pea island and Tubney — Tubba's island.

We leave the Kimmeridge Clay near Challow station and run on to the band of Gault Clay which extends on the transect to just short of Childrey. Flat and moist in appearance, it is covered by elm and willow, poplar and ash, and is still given over to pasture. In Victorian times and later, it provided, with the Kimmeridge Clay, claypits and brick-kilns, consequently one of the area's distinctive manufacturing activities at such places as Childrey, Challow, Marcham, Lyford, Garford, Drayton and Cumnor.

2

Beyond the Gault Clay a dramatic change takes place in soil, landscape and farming. Increasingly steeply one begins to ascend from the Vale towards the scarp slope of the chalk downland. On the light warmth of the greensand soil, arable and pastoral farming mix with orchards and market gardening, for this is the same soil type as at Harwell and Steventon Hill. It is a well-watered landscape, for at the chalk base rise a whole series of streams from springs which caused the development of spring-line settlements at such places as Blewbury, the Hendreds, Wantage, Letcombe Bassett, Childrey, Kingston Lisle and Woolstone.

The distinctive north Berkshire chalk outcrop with the Ridgeway at its summit once formed part of a sheep run of extensive proportions. In the late-ninteenth century beef herds took over some of the short-clipped grass, but the rolling backslope of the downland with its isolated farms and wide dry-valleys is now almost entirely ploughed to give huge fields of barley and wheat, divided from one another by hawthorn hedges or marching beech plantations. This is a landscape, in contrast to the Vale, so accurately described by Rudyard Kipling in his lines:

> We have no water to delight
> Our broad and brookless vales —
> Only the dew-pond on the height,
> Unfed, that never fails.

1

Nineteenth century Berkshire in a national economic setting

The nineteenth century saw tremendous economic change over all England; this was a period when man moved from a dispersed, rural and essentially agricultural society, into an urban, industrial and much more gregarious way of life. Although the rate of economic change varied from one region of England to another, no part of the country escaped the three-fold revolution which was making itself felt on society and the landscape; in this process Berkshire had a part to play. It is my intention here to sketch those broad economic trends which changed England between about 1780 and 1914, but also in the following chapters to illustrate some of the specific movements with detail and example taken from the Vale of the White Horse, and when relevant from elsewhere in Berkshire.

The three revolutions took place in approximate sequence in agriculture, industry and transport, but were not revolutions in the sense of rapid and complete change. They related rather to an evolution, having the overall effect of modifying the Englishman's way of life. The rural England of Sir Roger de Coverley could still be found in some parts of the country in 1800 or perhaps even 1850. Likewise the general character of England in 1800 could still be found in isolated areas a century later. In all probability north and west Berkshire fell into this last category as a region where "the tide of progress stirs but just enough to avert stagnation; where old-world customs and archaic forms of speech still linger and where men go about their daily tasks in a spirit of serene leisureliness." [1]

1 Travels Round our Village, E. G. Hayden

5

In Jethro Tull Berkshire had one of the greatest and earliest agricultural innovators. He was born at Basildon and farmed there, and also at Howberry Farm just over the Thames at Wallingford, but later in life at Prosperous Farm near Hungerford. *Horse-Hoeing Husbandry*, published in 1731, formed the basis of Tullian farming with the horse-hoe and the drill. The drill sowed in an even line and at a regular depth, and since the seed was no longer broadcast haphazardly it was possible to use the hoe between the lines to clean growing crops. Cultivation in this manner released previously untouched soil qualities and in its way helped make possible the later use of intensive arable farming techniques by such local farmers as Sir John Throckmorton at Buckland, Edward Loveden at Buscot and Philip Pusey at Pusey. Herein lay the essence of the agricultural revolution. Enclosure, selective animal breeding, drainage of farmland, fertilizing the soil, development of new crops and fresh techniques, intensive methods of husbandry both arable and pastoral, were all made possible, having the cumulative result of increasing yields and making farming more efficient. During the nineteenth century farm output rose gradually and helped provide much-needed food to feed the growing concentration of urban and industrial population in the coalfield and manufacturing areas of England. Many of these families had moved to the towns having been dispossessed of land through the movement to enclosure.

Industry ceased to be organized on the domestic putting-out basis, where a journeyman distributed and collected uncomplicated work from cottagers, and was developing instead in factories which in turn demanded a reliable, literate and very local labour supply; itself the mainspring of urbanisation. Cotton and woollen textiles, silk, iron founding, metal processing, engineering, the processing of linen and jute, hosiery and lace, the manufacture of all kinds of pottery, were concentrating production in factories. These manufactured items, cheap

Lancashire textiles, Yorkshire woollens and metal goods from midland England, found a growing market in the British Empire and elsewhere abroad. They were traded for industrial raw materials and foodstuffs, now badly needed to sustain our infant industrial society. Local economies based on the individual Berkshire market towns gradually grew into regional economies, and were to be transformed into a national economy. Local self-sufficiency developed into a regional economic inter-dependence — the industrial midlands and north became dependent upon the agricultural regions surrounding them, and they in turn upon manufacturers established elsewhere for their ploughs, implements and hand-tools which were enabling farm output to rise. As foreign countries underwent their own agricultural and industrial revolutions — the United States of America, Germany, France, the Low Countries — so the distinct national economies gave way in the later nineteenth century to an international economy.

The implication of international economic relations was not just the need and desire to trade, but also the ability to move manufactures and raw materials both internally and externally. The wooden sailing-ship gave way to the iron steam-vessel, but our transport revolution, like changes in farming and manufacturing, was a continuing process. River improvement on the Trent, Mersey, Severn and Thames led to development of a canal network. Heavy, bulky, low-value materials such as coal, ores, stone, building materials and timber, could now be moved cheaply but slowly. Improvements to the road system — bridging, turnpiking, macadamisation — helped speed up the road waggon, the mail and passenger coach. All in all, communications experienced improved speed, reliability, accessibility and safety. The development of railways in the earlier years of the century resulted in a reasonable system by 1845 to 1850, and, so far as goods were concerned, took over many of the functions previously carried out by river and canal barge, road waggon and coaster. To mid-Victorian England the railway seemed to be the ultimate stage in the evolution in the science of transportation; for now goods could be carried more quickly, in greater bulk, and moved directly from mine to factory, from factory to port, or from country market town to industrial centre. The development of the national economy was almost complete.

But were these the only important features of nineteenth-century England? Surely not, for along with the three great revolutions came accompanying social and welfare improvements and a tremendous expansion in the scope of government. Medical science advanced, hospitals were built, new techniques came into use, but some diseases were still endemic; dietary standards improved, but local dearths did occur; the general standard of living rose, but both urban and rural distress could be found; real incomes increased, but in many areas real poverty was very evident. Many people became better off in statistical terms, but at the same time the gulf between wealthy and poor widened and there developed an expanding industrial and agricultural proletariat, increasingly dependent upon the machine and the landlord; these elements of English social structure can clearly be seen in the story of nineteenth-century north Berkshire.

EXTRACT FROM AN ACCOUNT BOOK KEPT BY A VALE OF THE WHITE HORSE FARMER, 1805

	£	s	d
1293 eggs, at 2 for 1s	2	13	10
166 fowls, at 3s per couple	12	9	0
31 ducks, at 4s 6d per couple	3	9	9
22 geese, at 5s each	5	10	0
34 turkies, at 7s 6d each	17	15	0
	36	7	7
147 pigeons used in the house at 5s per dozen	3	1	3
550 sold at 5s per dozen	10	15	10½
	13	17	1½

2

Estates, rents, tithes and the poor rate

It is a natural tendency to associate the important farming activity in England with enterprise on the great and lesser estates. North Berkshire was covered pretty thickly with country seats, and at the end of the eighteenth century a whole host of gentry farmed local manors and estates, several having at the centre recently-built country mansions. It was said that "the pleasantness of the situation, salubrity of the air, and ready access to London" caused a whole string of big houses to be sited below the Corallian Limestone ridge from Buscot and Coleshill, through Faringdon and Hinton Waldrist as far as Cumnor and Wytham. Buscot Park was enthusiastically farmed by Edward Loveden, Sir John Throckmorton owned Buckland manor, Philip Pusey pioneered new techniques on the Pusey estate, Robert Southby was at Appleton, Sir Charles Saxton at Circourt near Denchworth, Sir George Bowyer occupied Radley Park and Adam Blandy kept the Kingston Bagpuize estate. On the other side of the Vale the Earl of Craven owned Ashdown Park, the Rev. J. Collins lived at Betterton House, the Rev. Philip Wroughton at Woolley Park, while Charles Dundas M.P. ran Barton Court near Abingdon.

About 1805 the total income from landed property, houses, mills, and other productive agricultural assets in Berkshire amounted to some £500,000, but substantial landowners in north Berkshire were relatively few. Of the more important were Edward Loveden, John Throckmorton, Philip Pusey, Lord Craven, and the Earl of Abingdon at Wytham Abbey. At this period they may each

9

have cleared £8,000 a year from their estates, and a few other large farms may have brought in an annual income of between £5,000 and £7,000. Nevertheless, the vast majority of yeomen farmers' incomes and those of the tenantry amounted normally to something between £50 and £400 a year.

Loveden's Buscot Park on the Thames near Faringdon was one of north Berkshire's most progressive estates. An early nineteenth-century writer described it as "a model estate fit for other landowners to copy, combining as it did utility with economy". The whole establishment was compact, comprising a semi-circular cart-lodge backing conveniently on to the oxen pens; the rick yard was close by, with implement houses to one side. Across the way, with ready access to the hay ricks, were animal pens for cattle, oxen, pigs, poultry, horses and sheep, while scattered nearby were sawpits, a carpenter's shop, the smithy, a dairy and brewhouse. That same writer concluded that Loveden's farm had suffered somewhat in efficiency through piecemeal development in comparison with Philip Pusey's estate which had recently been improved; it had been excellently but very expensively replanned. [1]

But this is not to give the idea of farming organised only on great estates, for at this time yeomen farmers and tenants abounded. Their rents helped to swell the incomes of the larger estate and were usually calculated upon the estimated income a small farm should produce. Where a landholding realised only £50 a year, the rent rarely exceeded sixpence (2½p) in the pound, but for a farm yielding £400 the rent would rise to 1s 6d (7½p) in the pound. From village to village rents varied, possibly according to soil quality; but they were also related to the benevolence of any particular landlord. Around 1800 moderately sized farms at Hanney could be let at 40s (£2.00) an acre for meadow, and 25s (£1.25) for arable land. Kingston Bagpuize and Buckland farms brought in a rent of 21s (£1.05) an acre, while Sparsholt and Childrey farmers paid 7s (35p) to 12s (60p) for downland pastures, 21s (£1.05)

1   Mavor

10

for middle lands on the greensand ledge while the rich Vale lands raised 30s (£1.50) an acre.

By far the highest rents I have encountered were paid for the Ock farmlands near Abingdon Common, where arable fetched 30s (£1.50) to 40s (£2.00) an acre, and particularly fine meadowland reached 50s (£2.50) to 70s (£3.50) an acre, but the picture over the whole area showed that everywhere downland rents were lower than charges made in the Vale. In terms of scale, downland sheep farms had of economic necessity to be extensive, but farm for farm annual rents were often no higher than on Vale farms, where half the number of acres constituted a large farm.

In addition to rents several other charges were frequently levied on tenants: probably those which caused most objection were tithes, and the old one-tenth of all farm goods appropriated by the church was normally paid with reluctance. It was normal for a farmer entering a new tenancy to make his bargain subject to tithes; sometimes a benevolent landlord made himself personally responsible for their payment, and they often amounted to about 4s (20p) in the pound of rent, but were by 1800 levied in cash rather than kind. Nevertheless high tithes in the richest dairy farming area of Berkshire's Vale could reach an additional 7s (35p) for each pound of rent.

With enclosure some villages were exonerated from tithes by Act of Parliament, and small parcels of land presented in lieu of their payment; Denchworth and Uffington were examples, but one odd custom was still maintained at Cumnor, where those parishioners who paid tithes to the incumbent claimed entertainment from him on the afternoon of Christmas Day. He was always to provide fine ale and beer made from four bushels of malt; two bushels of wheat to be made into bread, and half a hundredweight of cheese to go with this feast. But by 1800 an allowance of money was permitted in lieu of this lavish spread.

The Poor Rate was a further charge which countryfolk felt particularly heavily in time of agricultural depression. Figures taken from the *Parliamentary Returns for Berkshire* indicate that the cost of maintaining the needy

11

doubled between 1776 and 1804 and at Easter 1803 stood at £96,860, being raised from a rate of 4s 11d (24p) in the pound, but valuation varied from area to area and was seldom assessed on real rent. In the towns which had an efficient workhouse, the poor rate was usually lower than elsewhere. Wantage workhouse could cater for three hundred people but in 1803 had but seventy inmates. By its functioning the poor rate fell 2s 3d (11p) and was no more than 3s (15p) in the pound, while at Wallingford, where there was then no effective workhouse, rates were as high as 11s (55p) in the pound.

Abingdon's workhouse held both aged and children and was very badly sited near the town centre. Normally this "ill-contrived receptacle of poverty and destitution" held some eighty to one hundred people, and the inmates concentrated all their labour on sacking manufacture. One of the most efficiently-run houses appears to have been at Faringdon. Established in the reign of George III for the "better relief and employment of the poor", it was well conducted by the governor and governess, guardians and visitor. Children in large families were taken; the boys and girls being occupied by spinning worsteds until they could be put out to agriculture or into domestic service. Before its establishment Faringdon's poor rate was well over 10s (50p) in the pound, but by 1800 had fallen to a mere 4s (20p). In order to encourage thrift and saving there was considerable development of Friendly Societies in Berkshire throughout the nineteenth century. In time of illness or unemployment the Society would support members. In 1809 a Friendly Society was established at Wantage, in 1815 at Hungerford, in 1819 at Kingston Bagpuize, and in 1820 at Abingdon. It is pretty clear that our great-grandfathers were economically and socially not at all well off.

THE COMMUNAL COWHERD AT STANFORD-IN-THE-VALE

Before the common lands of the parish were enclosed those of the villagers who owned cows used to send them out to graze under the care of the parish cowherd. The animals were collected every morning by the winding of a horn; if this failed to bring them forth the cowherd would shout in the streets: 'Bring out your cow-cattle — turn 'um loose.' Throughout the day he guarded his meek charges, seeing that none strayed into the adjacent fields of corn; when milking time came he would gather them together, persuade them home again — it was little driving they needed — and announcing his arrival in the village by a second blast, he would consign them to their respective owners.

(*Islands of the Vale* by Eleanor Hayden)

3

Enclosing, draining and fertilising the land

That great period of change in English agriculture, from the old open field system of medieval days to the neat and relatively efficient enclosed fields of modern times, came in most north Berkshire villages between 1780 and 1830. There was certainly upheaval, but for rural areas to adopt the new methods of farming, rotations and selective breeding among them, enclosure was vital. By 1780 several villages were already enclosed. Hatford had lost its open fields as early as 1577, and at the end of James I's reign fences ringed some of Buscot's former common land, but the bulk of parishes were enclosed between 1770 and 1810. Aston Tirrold grew hedges in 1742, while many of the downland settlements, such as Ashbury, Childrey and Farnborough, were enclosed in the 1770's. But it was not until the early years of the nineteenth century that this movement spread to the villages of the Berkshire Vale. Wantage and Grove, Buckland, Lyford and Hanney were enclosed under the General Enclosure Act by 1804; shortly after 1804 followed Letcombe Regis, the Challows, Denchworth and Sparsholt: even as late as 1807 Fyfield, Appleton, Ardington, Chaddleworth and the Wittenhams remained essentially in that medieval state of farming, while Lockinge was not enclosed until 1853.

One would expect many farmers bitterly to oppose enclosure, but to some its benefits were patently obvious. Mr. Bushnell who farmed at Aston Tirrold objected not so much to actual enclosure but to the way his neighbours were carrying it out. Farmers who planted willow and osier sets to provide live hedges were wrong, he said, for although

15

fences were liable to be stolen by the poor, "hedges take up space, harbour birds and insects and very much shade the corn. I think the green land requires fencing." So if Bushnell had got his way we might have lost one of the characteristic features of the English landscape.

These newly enclosed fields varied greatly in size from one part of the north Berkshire to another. Fields on the downland chalk often reached one hundred acres each: sheep runs of an extensive kind. Even Mr. Brown at Idstone and various farms at Ashbury possessed several meadows of eighty acres, but in the Vale it was a different picture, for fields rarely exceeded twenty acres.

Just as the type of enclosure varied between downland and Vale, so did the type of cultivation. Possibly the seven-year rotation at Ashbury was exceptional but on the hills rotations were much longer than in the Vale. At Letcombe Bassett wheat was grown only one year in seven on the poor chalky soil, while on the richer greensand wheat took a four-year turn with clover, beans, and a season of fallow. Deep in the Berkshire Vale there was a four-year rotation, possibly typified by Hanney's where on the common fields a year of fallow was followed by wheat, beans and barley, while on enclosed land a green crop replaced the fallow. After enclosure notable improvements often occurred, but on land which remained in common ownership there was hardly any attempt to progress; the system defeated the objective.

Through much of the Vale, farmers attempted to drain their enclosed fields, led by that pioneer of agricultural improvement in the area, Edward Loveden. At Buscot he accomplished the task effectively by using Scott's mole plough which cost two guineas to buy, and was well recommended for the job. He put down brick drains, but these were expensive and most farmers who attempted to take his lead were forced to use stone drains and some rib drains — alder or heath filling the trench which permitted the surface water to drain off — so great was the cost of Loveden's method.

A further innovation which enclosure made possible was

a measure of irrigation. Although its value had been recognised from time immemorial its efficient use needed too much contrivance and science for many local farmers to summon, and in consequence it was still as yet little used. However, on Thames-side pastures problems were reduced and Loveden (Buscot), Throckmorton (Buckland) and Southby (Appleton) did attempt to conquer the problems irrigation posed. By 1808 Loveden was experimenting on a six-acre meadow at Buscot. He calculated his cost of irrigation at two guineas an acre and the main expense was for flooding the land; for the equivalent of an extra one inch of rainfall, yields increased by some fifty per cent.

As a result of his initiative Loveden could mow grass much earlier than on comparable pastures and, quite logically, claimed that cows fed on hay made from irrigated grass produced more milk. Watermeadows on a small scale extended for some distance along the Ock below Abingdon and on the Letcombe Brook near Wantage, while one hundred acres were effectively watered at Milton from the Mill stream, but an expensive scheme for irrigation at East Lockinge failed and was soon abandoned. The meadows were flooded by taking water from adjacent streams through a series of ducts, sluices and dams flooding the water meadow to a depth of about an inch. This protected grass from frost and encouraged growth by sedimentation often forcing it to a height of five or six inches. The flooding took place early in the year in order to provide an early bite for sheep and cattle in April. By the end of April the cattle had eaten the grass, and the subsequent growth was mowed for hay. From June to October cattle were pastured and from November the meadow was prepared for the next flood water. Floating the water meadows helped increase the number of animals which could be kept on farms and prevented the autumn slaughter of cattle and sheep; a characteristic of English farming since the middle ages.

At the opposite end of the scale the common fields remained undrained and water found its own way along the furrows to the nearest ditch. One pities the poor peasant who in a particularly wet season occupied the lowest strips of a village field.

In these days before artificial fertilisers, all manner of methods were used to raise the soil's richness, and again the enclosed land had an enormous advantage over the old open fields. Farmyard manure was not yet greatly used and Mr. Selwood, who in the 1790's farmed at Aldworth, was one of the first men to spread dung on his grassland; nevertheless folding sheep over crops was a very common alternative on the downland. Sheep flocks were hurdled on turnips, and this scheme was extended for use on barley. Francis Justice at Sutton Courtenay led the way for numerous farmers in the Vale by burning his bean stubble, the ashes being spread over the surrounding meadows. At Buckland and Buscot paring and burning (an ancient custom on the downs) improved fertility, while soot and soaper's ashes if spread over the cold and moister meadows were said to be most effective growth stimulants. As a top dressing to clover, grasses, turnips, vetch, and sometimes wheat, peat ashes were liberally spread on arable fields. As an indication of the use of this method of manuring one may quote the huge rise in value of Berkshire's peat-producing lands. In 1745 only £30 an acre could be obtained for them, but by 1800 they were fetching £300 and sometimes £400 an acre. In normal times a dressing of fifteen to twenty-five bushels per acre would cost the farmer about five shillings an acre. Peat, dug in May or June, was allowed to dry for three weeks during which farm workers turned the sods half-a-dozen times; then it was burnt in heaps, the fire often lasting as much as six weeks. Finally the ashes were removed to be stored for spreading over the land the following March. Commonly dug at Marcham, it was used right along the Ock, especially on clover, while at Milton coal ashes from local works were considered a fair substitute and scattered over growing crops. Around the Berkshire market towns malt dust was used to quicken plants' growth. Easily obtainable from the countless brewhouses, it was hand spread at about thirty bushels to an acre, then harrowed-in with the grain seeds. Its use is recorded at Marcham, Shefford and Aldworth, but was probably more widespread than this.

At one period just before 1800 it was found to be economical to move street manure by barge from London to spread over the riparian lands, while woollen tags and rags from the Cotswolds and Oxfordshire woollen towns were applied to farmland at Marcham and elsewhere in the Vale, but as yet only the most progressive farmers were ploughing in their green crops.

To some farmers enclosure of land was an enormous opportunity to improve their methods and to experiment — often only on a modest scale — but the results they achieved were striking. Nevertheless, several decades passed before their techniques became generally used.

COLLECTING THE HARVEST, 1910

Rain was threatening, and the entire household had evidently been pressed into service. At one waggon the farmer was pitching, at another his wife was doing likewise, while the servant-maid led the horses . . . In the same field were ten waggons; the season was far advanced, and every horse and hand had been turned on . . . Backwards and forwards they crept to the verge of the golden stubble, beyond which blazed a patch of mustard; some were returning empty to be loaded again, others were making heavy progress towards the ricks in the corner. It was a picture of plenty, of peace, and the healthful toil that sweetens repose . . . I do not know whether in other parts of England the corn is still carried by the light of the harvest-moon. In the district round (West Hendred) this has not been done for many years. The days are over when employers and employed used to work until two o'clock in the morning in order to clear the field before rain fell.

(*Turnpike Travellers* by Eleanor Hayden)

4

Ploughing, drilling and threshing

Over much of England the eighteenth century had been a period of noteworthy agricultural changes in which the methods of farming made considerable advances. In so far as the White Horse Vale was concerned, the movement towards improvement and higher technical efficiency in the rest of southern England made its impact felt upon this corner of Berkshire. For instance, on many local farms, the techniques of ploughing had certainly come a long way from the old wooden breast-plough which just pared off the turf of a meadow, preparing it "for the most slavish work of husbandry". By 1800 the furrow plough drawn by horse-teams, but still here and there by oxen, was a prominent part of the countryside landscape. The Berkshire two-wheeled plough had been called "a heavy, clumsy instrument, better adapted for trenching than the uses required", but in various regions of the Vale having a sticky-clay soil it was worthwhile. At this time the Norfolk and Suffolk Iron Swing Plough was frequently used for the heavier clays in the Vale of the White Horse. Although recommended for use only on very wet clays, and said to be otherwise virtually useless because it was so light, it did help point the way towards change in farming techniques, and its use did achieve a loosening of the farming community's inflexible attitudes.

This problem of obtaining a plough sufficiently heavy for the wet clay-soils was felt over most of the country. A Newbury farmer put five horses to one plough but he was hard pressed to complete an acre in a day because the implement was not strong. In the 1780's it was usual to have teams of four or five horses to plough on heavy or stony land, but only a pair of animals were needed for loose or light soil. Some farmers, for instance farmer Stacey at

21

Abingdon, made use of oxen, and Sir John Thockmorton at Buckland worked three pairs of beasts. There was a pair at Radley and Mr. Morland at West Ilsley kept several teams to plough downland slopes.

For Buscot soils Loveden had ploughs made in Leicestershire, having sometimes one but latterly two shares as two-share ploughing became more usual in the locality, especially on the drier slopes of the Berkshire Downs where the clay-with-flint soil was less clinging. At Letcombe Bassett a two-share plough with two very widely-set wheels could be used with safety on all but steepest gradients, and these were manufactured for local farmers by Messrs. Radway of Cirencester and much approved of in downland Berkshire; their great disadvantage was that they needed four horses to haul them. Fortunately in 1800 Mr. William Plenty developed a new type of iron plough which he manufactured in Newbury; it satisfied a wide demand in west Berkshire.

Now that settled forms of ploughing existed in the area, cast-iron plough-shares were becoming common for their cheapness and durability; Mr. W. Morland at West Ilsley invented replaceable stocks or points for his sets and they attracted considerable attention when they were exhibited at the *Berkshire Agricultural Society's* meeting in 1804, and subsequently were widely used.

In that same area a vast ploughing contraption was in use on higher parts of the downs — the nine-share plough — and elsewhere on the chalky, light soils the five-share, seven-share, and nine-share plough eventually became quite common. This monster plough belonging to Mr. Jethro Tull of West Ilsley was used by him in an unconventional manner. First he manured the land, ploughed it, then rolled it, finally sowing his seeds broadcast. The plough was then passed over the sown land causing the grain to grow in drills. The implement was a useful but uneconomic substitute for the drill, and as yet there were few seed drills in the country. Among these Berkshire landowners who did possess drills were John Throckmorton at Buckland and Mr. O. Williams, M.P.

who used to sow grains and pulses. It was actually in Berkshire that the drill was developed and first used, by Jethro Tull, who was born and buried at Basildon. His Ilsley farm was described by William Cobbett in *Rural Rides*, written some years after Tull's death, as being on loam ground, free from wetness, and needing no water furrows.

Cobbett noted that in the neighbourhood of Jethro Tull's farm were large tracts of turnips, clean (fallow) land, stubbles ploughed up early, ploughing with oxen, and a very large and singularly fine flock of sheep. "The land, stock, fences, and implements, all do credit to the owner." On the farm the first seed drill was used and here Jethro Tull practised his husbandry and wrote that famous book *Horse-Hoeing Husbandry* to which the farmers of England owe so much.

The threshing machine was another innovation of the period and Berkshire farmers soon had a fair number. This activity was the first major operation on the farm to be fully mechanized. Although a primitive threshing machine was reported to have been in use in the second quarter of the seventeenth century, the use of water-powered and horse-powered threshers was not common until after 1815, and then largely in northern England where there was an increasing dearth of harvest-time temporary labour. By the mid-1840's steam power began to replace horse and water as the motive power and the threshing machine spread quickly to all but the remotest parts of England; by the late 1860's horse power was no longer a feature of modern threshing machines, and farmers increasingly set up their own steam engines either in the form of a static plant, or by the use of a traction engine. In terms of innovation the threshing machine was doubly important, for it was much more efficient in every respect than the use of flail and winnowing fan, but also released labour and storage space which enabled farmers to diversify activity into animal rearing.

In the early part of the century a threshing machine at Ashbury was turned by four horses and produced twelve quarters of grain a day — but this was low yielding and costly to work. At West Ilsley, on Morland's farm, a six-horsepowered machine, which had cost thirty guineas, produced twelve bushels a day and cut the chaff at the same time, while Mr. B. Morland at Abingdon used an adapted two-horsepower implement which threshed five quarters in eight to nine hours. Sir John Throckmorton used a machine highly spoken of by local farmers which cost fifty guineas from a Norwich firm, and the Rev. Robert Symonds at neighbouring Hinton Waldrist soon purchased a similar machine. While threshing was in progress there was a maximum demand for labour on the farms and consequently the daily rate of pay was higher than during the remainder of the year. For the man who fed the sheaves into the machine was half-a-crown (12½p) a day, the girl or boy who handed to him and unbound the sheaves had 8d (3p) a day. The man who sifted and riddled the corn had 2s 6d (12½p) a day plus a free beer or cider ration. [1]

One important local aid to technological change on the farm was the *Berkshire Agricultural Society*, which was formed in 1794, and intended partly to disseminate to farmers available information about the newly developed techniques, and partly to act as a discussion forum for men with common interests. The Society was set up on an extensive scale with eight district sub-committees which made frequent reports about farming methods in their areas. But unfortunately the Society did not flourish, and came to be used for party-political purposes at elections. Farmers tired of the in-fighting and of its involved organisation; one by one members withdrew. [2] Sufficient farmers agreed to subscribe their guinea a year for it to get under way again with more modest organization and the Society was re-constituted in 1800; it planned ploughing matches, awarded prizes for the best sheep-shearer, the best bull-producer, for the best cow, lamb, and pig, and ran several competitions for honey production, which at the time was a common local activity. One typical Abingdon

---

1   WHC p.62
2   WHC p.183

24

bee-keeper frequently cleared £27 a year with his bees, and from West Ilsley hives often yielded 42 lbs of high quality honey a season. Even in Victorian times bee-keeping was in some Vale villages pursued on a commercial scale; honey was in itself an important crop, but was also of consequence in making mead.

The Agricultural Society also took the initiative in establishing wool fairs at Wantage and Newbury and offered an award for the cottager rearing the largest family without resort to parish relief. [3]

3   See p.48

TIMBER AUCTION AT KINGSTON BAGPUIZE

To be sold at the Hind's Head, Kingston, Berks., 398 fine large maiden Elms, standing at Kingston Bagpuize and Bullock's Pits, near excellent roads, near the River Thames, and the wharfs at Newbridge, Oxford, and Abingdon, where barges are constantly loaded for the London Markets.

(Jackson's Oxford Journal November 1st 1817)

5

Fish, fruit and timber

Mr. Edward Loveden's Fish House at Buscot was something of a novelty. It was intended to prevent poachers stealing his trout, and he developed and erected the building on a peninsula of land between Buscot Island and the main channel of the Thames. At this point gratings of sufficient mesh allowed water to pass through, but the fish were forced to drop into an enclosed tank eight feet below the building. Access to it was by way of a locked trap-door and each morning one of Loveden's men would collect the previous night's catch. Fish production in the Vale of the White Horse was just one of those items which, as the nineteenth century dawned, made a perceptible contribution to the area's agricultural output. Among the others were timber and fruit growing, each speciality often confined to a specific district which soon became well known for the production of the crop.

But to return to Buscot: here Loveden constructed lakes, the largest covering over thirty acres, which frequently furnished him with high quality pike of up to 20 lbs each. To have a regular supply of fresh fish was an important asset for country gentlemen, and Loveden supplied not only his own table, but those of households far afield in the surrounding counties. Soon those lakes became well known for succulent eels, for carp, tench, and high quality perch and trout. But fish in quantity was taken from other streams. The River Ock gave up very good pike, some perch and a little gudgeon, with roach, dace and crayfish. The Thames at Abingdon yielded high quality eels, taken from the river sometimes by eel spears — a slender fork in the shape of a hand fixed to a long handle and with metal fingers for catching the eels. Sometimes an eel crook was used for flicking eels from the water, but this method was crude and very slow. The greatest catch came from eel traps, long willow baskets often called putcheons, up to fifty inches from end to end, which were baited with rabbit meat.[1] Excellent dace and gudgeon came from the Thames at Wallingford, and all down the river numerous fish weirs had been set up. Although helpful for the fish trade, they were impossible for the increasing navigation on the river. Nevertheless above Oxford there remained many weirs from which came barbel, pike, and at Buckland, trout. Around 1800 the average market price for Thames fish was about a shilling (5p) a pound and this was high enough to encurage sufficient production, not only to furnish trade in the local towns, but to provide for an export of fish to the London markets.

Alexander Pope commented that the swift Kennet was for silver eels renowned . . but trout too were taken in quantity about Newbury. Often individual fish measured up to forty-five inches in length and weighed over 15 lbs. In the locality, along with eels, they were esteemed a delicacy and consequently fetched a suitably high price.

At this period even the modest flows of the Childrey, Letcombe, and Ginge brooks yielded fish of commercial importance. Crayfish were taken from the Mill brook near Milton and Sutton Courtenay and sold in local markets, while in the upper reaches of the other brooks they were caught largely for personal consumption by cottagers of water-side villages. In addition a quantity of fish taken each year in the Berkshire Vale was marketed at local towns and more distant centres.

All over the Vale apple and pear orchards were widespread, here and there for cider making, often specially to provide the six-quart ration for men working in the corn fields, the drink being carried from the farm in small hand-barrels of wood and copper called cider costrels. Eating and keeping apples came from most villages and some were sold in London, carried there by road waggon or

1 Many examples of river-fishing implements may be seen in the Folk Museum, Gloucester.

Thames barge. Wantage had apple and cherry orchards, and once a year a cherry fair. Cherries of more than local repute were grown at Great Coxwell, West Hanney, Blewbury, and a very large production from the warm greensands in the Hagbourne and Harwell districts. The year's crop was sent either to London, Oxford or Bath for marketing according to their situation, and in a few villages a liqueur was produced when black heart cherries were infused with brandy, [2] but usually the fruit was eaten dessert, while here and there the gum from cherry trees was collected and made into glue.

Apple orchards were in abundance surrounding virtually every Vale village, but nowhere to the same extent as at Milton. Here a Mr. Hopkins had a twenty-two acre apple and cherry plantation which contained over 540 trees, and was believed to be the largest single orchard in the county. Over at Wytham and in the villages close to Oxford that had the correct aspect and soil, strawberries were widely grown and marketed. At Buscot Park Loveden perfected his canvas awnings which helped protect fruit and blossom from frost and blight.

The ample and varied timber resources of the Vale were of great commercial use in north Berkshire; of them the oak was highly important on the clays and loams of the region; they flourished in Bagley Wood, in the neighbourhood of Radley, and oak plantations were inaugurated at Milton, while about 1810 several fine specimens from Sparsholt fetched £70 each. Sixty pounds to £65 was considered a normal price for trees from this village. The timber was used for a variety of purposes, for instance to make field gates and fencing posts, as a house building material, for cutting into roof shingles, and for making domestic furniture. Oak bark was in constant demand in the market towns for use in the tanning trade. It has been suggested that local tannery failures between 1809 and 1811 recorded in *The Reading Mercury* may have been the result of an inadequate re-planting policy so that supply of oak increasingly lagged behind the tannery requirements.

[2] Recipe p.40

In Loveden's ash plantation at Buscot poles cut from seven-year-old trees were actively traded to farmers in the vicinity. Although they were useful agriculturally, ash had by 1810 become mere hedgerow trees, and were frequently pollarded. In the wetter areas of the Vale and in the Newbury area alders were cultivated by farmers, often being planted on boggy areas where little else would flourish. The trees yielded timber as handles for rakes, prongs, brooms, and mops. Hundreds of dozens went annually to the west of England from alder trees with eight or nine years' growth. Between 1780 and 1800 oak, elm, and ash prices doubled. The price rise was caused by stripping woodlands on estates when new owners took over. They sold the wood to pay accumulated debts, but nevertheless some fresh plantations were started. At the opposite extreme was Bagley Wood, the largest woodland area in north Berkshire, where grew fine quality oak, but one commentator suggested that its owner, St. John's College, was not making the best use of this valuable resource.

Hazel and coppice wood was an important source of fuel before transport innovations allowed coal to be brought into the Vale at a suitably low cost. Hazel plantations on the downs which had been allowed to thrive for seven or ten years sold for between £6 and £9 an acre, while hazel cut every ten years in Wytham Abbey's wood sold in Oxford for the equivalent of £10 an acre. From the better soil at Radley hazel became fit in seven years and at market could realise up to £12 an acre. At numerous downland villages and in south Berkshire ash furnished timber for hoops and broom handles and cheap furniture manufacture. From Compton through Farnborough along to Lambourn, winter employment was provided for the poor, and for women, by preparing the ash for transport to the capital. About 1810 one hundred and twenty hoops in a middling bundle (hoops which furnished the middle part of baskets) fetched seven shillings. Sent by Thames barge at 5d (2p) a bundle they were sold to London dealers in lots of sixty bundles. When they travelled by road waggon a load could fetch five guineas (£5.25p) with another guinea

30

(£1.05p) charged on top for carriage. At this time the truism was quoted that a willow will purchase a horse before oak will buy him a saddle, and the fast-growing willow was widely cultivated, rather like the alder, in the wet, marshy parts of north Berkshire beside the Thames and in the low-lying Vale. Willow trunks were taken by barge from Lechlade to London — another of Loveden's enterprises — and were sold at between 2s 6d (12½p) and 3s 6d (17½p) a foot. Laths, five-barred gates, hurdles, poles, all of consequence on farms, were likewise cut and made in the district. Poles cut after eight years' growth fetched 1s 8d (8p) to 2s 6d (12½p) a pair at sixteen to twenty feet in length. Shoots were taken off to basket makers, and some wood from pollarded willows was made into ladies' hats. The winnowing fan, a large shallow basket with two handles, used for shaking and then tossing grain and chaff to the wind to separate the grain after it had been threshed with a flail, was usually made from willow woven on to an ash foundation, and even down to 1900 formed a useful piece of threshing equipment on many small farms.

Lord Tennyson noted that here and there in Berkshire the Thames was "streaming thro' his osier'd aits," and beside the river for much of its length these osiers grew quickly. Withy-willow beds were planted near Newbridge and Kingston Bagpuize, and by Loveden at Buscot. From them the osier planted in February and March would produce revenue of some £8 by the second year, the crop being sold to basket makers chiefly as white rods. There were three recognised types of willow rod. Green rods could be cut at any time of the year for use in cheap baskets; brown rods were taken in winter and stored for later use, while white rods were cut when the sap was rising in spring, and stored in water for ease of peeling. Pulling each rod through a stripping brake effectively removed the bark, but also gave rise to *Stripping the Willow* as a folk dance.

Stripping and preparing the osier rods occupied women and children in spring; they were paid about 2½d (1p) a bolt, a bundle forty-two inches in girth. So this was yet another way in which casual income came to localised parts of the Berkshire Vale.

AN OLD CHARM USED IN BUTTER MAKING

Churn, butter, churn!
Come, butter, come!
Peter stands at our gate,
Waiting for a butter-cake.
Churn, butter, churn!
Come, butter, come!

6

Butter, cheese and milk

In the first half of the nineteenth century agricultural enterprise in the Vale of the White Horse was widely characterised by extensive dairying, in some districts to the exclusion of any other speciality, partly the result of the heavy damp soil conditions existing over the Vale. About 1810 it was estimated that there were over three thousand dairy cattle between Shrivenham, Faringdon and Abingdon. Long-horned animals brought from Warwickshire and Oxfordshire formed many herds. While quality of milk was relatively high, the quantity was small, but near Abingdon cows from Yorkshire combined quantity and quality in yields, and at several villages richer farmers bought in animals from as far afield as Northumberland and Alderney, the latter giving especially good milk and a high butterfat content. Edward Loveden on the Buscot Estate frequently bred his own stock but also bought Scottish heifers two years old for around six guineas apiece. Some he kept for milk, others he fattened and sold a year later for between £10 and £12 a beast. One very finely-proportioned bull which was said to have bred perfect animals was bought by Loveden off Jethro Tull for forty-five guineas.

Close to the north Berkshire towns cows were kept for milk to make butter. A good wholesale price was between 1s (5p) and 1s 3d (6p) a pound, while about 1812 consumers normally paid 1s 3d (6p) to 1s 6d (7½p) a pound for the product. Much butter was used directly on the farm and by villagers; some found its way to Oxford and local markets, while still more was moved to London. The fertile riparian land between Radley and Wytham was said to produce the best butter in the area, but generally any meadowland bordering the Thames or Ock was conducive to a high butterfat content in milk and so fine butter. Until about the end of the nineteenth century butter making and dairy work had been the prerogative of the young women in a family — the traditional dairy maids. They were responsible for milking the cows by hand in the fields, carrying milk into the dairy and working it into butter and cheese. They used shallow cream skimmers — wooden dishes about six inches across — and scoops — ladles with small holes to permit milk to drain off — to separate the cream. These items were always hand made from best sycamore wood as it neither stained nor flavoured the butter; so were the decoratively designed butter prints, used for marking pats of butter. The swan and cow motifs were traditional designs, but variations frequently indicated butter from particular sources and acted as farm trade marks for their products. [1]

Large quantities of cheese came from the Vale, and at Buscot Loveden built warehouses on his Thames wharf to store them. From the surrounding areas, which included parts of Wiltshire, Oxfordshire and Gloucestershire, as well as north Berkshire, between two thousand and three thousand tons of cheese were collected annually (1809). [2] There were roughly ten cheeses to the hundredweight, so that even in mediocre seasons Loveden handled nearly half a million cheeses, the bulk of them being transferred in spring and summer down river by London Cheesemongers. About a thousand tons of cheese were made annually in the Berkshire Vale, usually of the Gloucester type, and so great was the demand for milk to make them that various complaints arose from townsfolk, who said it was quite impossible for them to buy sufficient cream to dilute their tea. Loveden used the latest devices, among them Garnett's patented press; also a wooden container, rather like half-a-beer-barrel in shape and fixed to a pair of wheels, to carry the cheese-milk around.

On other farms more ancient methods sufficed, and at

1 Examples of butter-making equipment can be seen at the Oxford and County Museum, Woodstock and at the Museum of English Rural Life, Reading.
2 Mavor p.375

Snowswick Farm near Buscot Mr. Pike made cheeses of a pineapple shape which were said to possess a peculiar delicacy and richness of flavour. The whole family worked the curds by hand, pressing them into flower-pot shaped wooden moulds. The resulting cheese was then removed to be suspended from rafters hanging in a fairly narrow mesh net which gave them their characteristic shape; they were later rubbed thoroughly with salt, then soaked in brine. Each cheese normally weighed five pounds and on that farm about two tons were produced annually, or, put another way, they made between nine hundred and a thousand cheeses each year. On most Vale farms the cheese presses could be seen standing in the kitchen. Some had winches which applied pressure through a wooden box containing stones and all manner of heavy scrap-metal. This was lowered on to the cheese beneath and squeezed out moisture. Occasionally one would come across these latest presses set up in pairs worked from the same winch.

So far as size of dairy herds were concerned there is poor information. It is recorded that Mr Gearing of Coleshill on the Earl of Radnor's estate kept a hundred head of cattle, reputedly the largest herd in the Vale, but the average herd contained about forty milking cows.

In addition to dairying in the Vale, beef cattle were fattened and Loveden kept Scottish beasts, which he fed on cut hay through most of the year. Six weeks before they were to be sold they received a special, but expensive, ration of linseed mixed with cut hay, which Loveden considered to be far better than mere oilseed. One of the largest beef animals and of considerable fame in the region was owned by Mr Tompkins at Abingdon who exhibited it locally as a natural curiosity. Francis Justice of Sutton Courtenay measured and painted the animal so that some detail of its shape could be retained for posterity. In height it was six feet and six inches; from nose to the top of the tail measured thirteen feet, eight inches; while from its knee to the ground was sixteen inches. It was of the short-horned Yorkshire breed and came from Shropshire. By report when Tompkins first had the animal it drank a barrel of water a day (twenty to twenty-four gallons) and was fed on barley meal with cut chaff. Later a pint of flax seed was boiled with water to form a jelly, and most of Tompkin's best animals were fed on this rich diet. It was stated, for the sake of the record, that Tompkins purchased the beast in November 1805 from Mr Warner of Coventry for eighty guineas, and sold it to Mr Bostock of Bath, in February 1807, for one hundred and thirty guineas.

TWO BERKSHIRE TITHE BARNS

The largest barn in this country, and which must have been built at enormous expence, is that belonging to the Manor of Cholsey, Lord Kensington's. It is 101 yards long, 18 yards wide, and is supported by 36 pillars of stone, each a yard square. On one of these pillars is the following inscription, which records a fact perhaps unique in the annals of agriculture. 'In this barn James Lansley threshed for Mr Joseph Hopkins 5 qrs 7½ lb of wheat in 13 hours, on March 15, 1747'. This extraordinary thresher was in his 93d year in 1805, and was as remarkable for his longevity, considering the business he followed, as for his performance in it. It seems he had two men to assist him in placing the ears of corn under his flail, and removing the straw; yet the feat is still astonishing, though well authenticated. At Great Coxwell, near Faringdon, is another large barn, though far inferior to the above. It is 148 feet long and 48 feet wide, and is a very fine piece of masonry, of vast strength, built by the abbots of Beaulieu, to whom it formed a grange.

(*General Survey of the Agriculture of Berkshire*
by William Mavor)

See WHC pp.141-2.

7

Weights, Measures and the Winchester bushel

Millers, farmers, dealers, factors and all middlemen connected with agriculture were in confusion. The period was the turn of the eighteenth century, and the problem was over weights and measures. North Berkshire's markets had by custom always sold grain in measure rather than weight, a system which itself was irregular in application and often quite unfair in its result. When a double criterion of measure came to be used the confusion was complete. By law the standard bushel was fixed at eight gallons but in the conservative rural areas of the Vale the bushel was by custom nine gallons. Everywhere far from the market towns corn jobbers forcibly maintained this substantial differential, reaping a large and illegal profit for their own pockets. Matters went from bad to worse. Somehow, someone had to attempt to halt this chaos in trade. One man acting by himself would accomplish little, and even when groups of more powerful landowners tried to standardise measures they always met combinations of corn jobbers specifically established to prevent general use of the legal bushel: commercial anarchy took the day.

There was one brave farmer — who also happened to be a magistrate: he was adamant in his determination to sell grain only at the legal eight-gallon bushel, but when week after week his agent failed to get any bids in markets, even he was forced to admit defeat and to return to the customary Berkshire measure.

The more enlightened agricultural improvers found the situation intolerable. They too tried to set the eight-gallon standard and hoped local farmers would follow them. In this respect John Throckmorton, Edward Loveden and Philip Pusey often succeeded where others failed for they were able to meet the combination of jobbers by sheer volume of trade alone. Nevertheless in the Vale of the White Horse, far removed from the local commercial centres, the nine-gallon bushel persisted; the farmers there seemed unable, or unwilling, to follow the lead of other men; consequently the grain speculators continued to dwell upon them. At Wantage and Faringdon markets the nine-gallon bushel was maintained well into the nineteenth century but at Abingdon a double measure came into use. The market's custom was always to use nine gallons and the corn merchants and malsters continued to reap surplus profit by selling wheat and malt out of the town in the legally established Winchester bushel.

Oddly enough, by 1812 the standard bushel had come to be accepted in other parts of the region — such places as Market (East) Ilsley, Hungerford, Lambourn and Wallingford — but even here it only applied to the grain trade. The Vale alone remained unwilling to comply; here and there wheat was even sold by the load of five quarters.

But *Jackson's Oxford Journal* reported a meeting at the Bear Inn, Wantage, in September 1817 to establish a pitched market for corn. Mr. Goodlake commented that he had helped "equalisation of measure" in the area "by the establishment of the Winchester bushel, which was not only adopted in the Town and Market of Wantage, but also in the neighbouring Towns of Abingdon and Faringdon". A few days earlier the same newspaper reported the Court Leet Jury's seizure in Abingdon Market of 101 lbs of butter deficient in weight; and on the two preceding market days the same Jury seized 56 lbs of butter. The whole consignment was condemned the next day in the Guildhall and distributed to the poor. [1]

The local application of other measures of length and quantity was often more standardised. For building, hedging, ditching and road mending the perch or pole of

---

[1] A complete set of local standard measures, dated 1826, may be seen in the County Hall, Abingdon.

eighteen feet was normal, but more precise distances were measured by the statute pole of sixteen and a half feet. Wood purchased for fencing and building was paid for by the foot and the load, while underwood — a valuable fuel before the canal was completed — was sold by the cord (the amount of rope taken to tie a bundle) and by the load, another quite arbitrary and wholly irregular standard.

For calculating rents and tithes landlords nearly always used statute acres, but for less accurate measurements the common and field acre were employed. These varied so widely that in some parishes the field acre was greater, in others smaller, than the statute acre. Not only did measures vary from parish to parish, but also between town and village and from county to county. To some extent the system of weights suffered from the same problems as did measures, but everywhere magistrates were vigilant to detect false weights and liquid measures and to a certain degree their task was easier, although village shops sold sea coal by the chaldron and pit coal by the hundred and ton — even in inns justice in measure and purity was rarely done. One man who fought against and was violently outspoken about these dual standards and abuses in the weights and measures system was Charles Dundas, Member of Parliament for Berkshire, and well he might speak against them for some of the worst abuses existed in his own constituency. Indeed he sought legislation to standardise and enforce a uniform system and went so far as to condemn measure as a thoroughly bad criterion of value. Of course he was quite right.

A RECIPE FOR MAKING BRANDIED CHERRIES

To a quart of the best brandy put a pound of Morella cherries and a pound of white sugar candy; tie it over with bladder and leather.

(Turnpike Travellers by Eleanor Hayden)

8

Hops, lavender, orchards and watercress

Parish records, contemporary books, trade magazines, directories and local newspapers frequently offer detailed and fairly lengthy accounts of crops and farming methods current in the nineteenth century; their information gives us a valuable picture of conditions on the land and helps reconstruction of the agricultural sequence in the early part of the century.

In the nineteenth century hops were grown more extensively in north Berkshire than today. Small hop grounds existed at East Hagbourne and near Kingston Bagpuize, while there was a ten-acre garden at Faringdon. Manor Farm at East Hagbourne had three hop kilns, but only one oast house remains today. However, numerous notes pencilled on chutes tell of past crops gathered in the village. "Finished hopping September 16th. 1868", runs one inscription, 10,013 bushels being picked, while in 1874 the yield fell to 9,370 bushels and in 1877 to 9,110 bushels. A fairly steady decline ensued and four years later in 1881 just under 5,000 bushels were collected. Although further references exist to crops grown in the 1890's, continued cultivation of hops in any big way soon died out. The foundations of the other two oast houses are still there to be seen, and within the existing brick and timber kiln are the boarded-up boiler, the slatted floor through which the warm wood smoke passed up to dry the hops, and, in another compartment, two circular holes high in the roof marking where the twelve-feet-long hop pockets were fixed for filling. Most of their produce was sent straight to the brew houses in the towns especially Wallingford, but at that time many village households made their own beer. At Lockinge, for instance, it was the custom to make a brew at the time of the village feast. Villagers advertised their wares by hanging boughs over their doorways, but stricter laws put an end to this amateur illicit brewing. To avoid detection by visiting excisemen villagers even hid hops and malt in the church tower. [1]

Woad was grown on some establishments around Wantage early on in the nineteenth century and was well valued by dyers, usually fetching good market prices. Whether sown by drill or broadcast, often in August, it was always hoed about three weeks later, then thinned until the plants were six inches apart. Each season up to four crops, each of diminishing value, were reaped and finally sheep put on the land, for it was thought that woad helped cure footrot.

Some hemp and flax grew in the Vale country, the flax being fed to cattle mixed with seed or oilcake, the hemp going to matting works in Abingdon and Wantage. Similarly dill was sown in March and scythed in September to make hay, or in full bloom for seed purposes. Dill seed usually yielded two to three quarters an acre and was sold off the farm at around 50s (£2.50) a quarter, so it was only a moderately lucrative crop and normally was mixed with barley or potatoes and fed to fatten hogs.

Here and there lavender was grown commercially and was often visible in rows of bushes some four feet apart. It ripened in July, and women and local children were employed to cut the heads, bundle them, then send them to the still-houses in baskets for distillation by coal or coke. Park Place near Henley became well known for possessing extensive lavender distilleries and the price fetched by lavender oil could reach 70s (£3.50) or 80s (£4.00) a pound, but in years of plenty it was more usually around 18s (90p) a pound.

It was Sir Robert Weston who brought clover from Brabant to England in 1645 and in the nineteenth century

1 WHC p.167.

42

the crop was grown throughout the Vale of the White Horse. Being planted at 14 lbs of seed an acre this innovation, coupled with transport improvements, eventually reduced hay prices from £3 to under £1 a load. Clover was later grown specifically for cattle grazing.

Mr. Jethro Tull at East Ilsley pioneered the growth of rye grass in the locality. Although nutritionally poor, it gave a cheap early bite and when sown with white dutch-clover was fed to horses. Records relate that sainfoin, which Jethro Tull favoured in his *Horse-Hoeing Husbandry*, was grown at Stanford-in-the-Vale, Ilsley, Fawley, Shefford and Pangbourne, generally on land for corn, while lucerne, another of Jethro's crops, was quite often cut and carried to horses and cattle between May and Michaelmas. One acre of lucerne, Tull claimed, would maintain double the number of cattle that would meadowland. Although it was introduced from France in 1653 the only instances of its growth locally in the nineteenth century was by the Rev. Dr. Hughes at Uffington, and at Sutton Wick, near Abingdon.

Orchard crops probably grew more plentifully in nineteenth-century north Berkshire than today, for then almost every village was encircled by fruit trees. The 1844 Tithe map of West Hanney shows orchards on a scale not evident today. South of the church a paddock is named specifically the Cherry Orchard. Although numerous apple and pear orchards covered the warm sands of the region surprisingly little cider was made from them. One commentator noted how badly these orchards were kept, bearing he thought, so little comparison with Somerset's well-kept trees. Naturally all the best apples were marketed in London and were moved there by Thames barge or road waggon, but now and again blight so ravaged the crop (on one occasion American blight spoilt trees right up to Oxford) that there were few exports outside the immediate vicinity of the orchards.

Cherries grew particularly well at Blewbury, West Hanney, Hagbourne, Harwell and the Coxwells, while wood from the trees was used for turning and by carpenters, once more stressing the importance of interrelations between agriculture and cottage industry. Mr. Hopkins, the skilled carpenter at Milton, particularly desired apple wood and he made furniture of a high quality from it. There were without doubt countless other instances of this kind all over north Berkshire.

Watercress has been grown in a number of Vale villages at the spring line of the Berkshire Downs perhaps for almost three hundred years. When Thomas Hardy wrote *Jude the Obscure* in 1894 he gave Letcombe Bassett the name Cresscombe, making it pretty clear that the crop was grown in the village then. Other villages soon followed Letcombe's lead and beds were cut at Ashbury, Childrey, Ginge, West Hendred and Blewbury. Of the watercress beds at the foot of the Berkshire Downs, and there were at least six of them in the nineteenth century, Letcombe was the best known. From the source of the Letcombe brook the beds extended downstream in a deep and fairly wide valley. Terraces formed by mudbanks and timber broke the course of the brook so that the water flowed by a series of steps. Today, the cress is grown in the ponds which are formed by these artificial banks. The main ponds in the upper waters cover about three acres, but further down they have been neglected and are no longer used. Nevertheless watercress cultivation still extends for nearly half-a-mile along the brook. Cutting often starts in February, but the date varies with the weather: the wetter the winter the earlier cress can be taken, for the warmer water flowing from the chalk encourages early growth. When the mayfly arrives in the beds, damaging the leaves, cutting comes to an end; this is often in April.

THE VILLAGE ROAD WAGGON DEPARTS
FOR LONDON

The principal weekly event in the village was the departure of the road waggon for London, and its return. It was despatched, laden with passengers and country produce, by the one tradesman of the place. An eye-witness told how the waggon and its four huge horses used to start at five o'clock on a Sunday evening. 'It stood on the green outside the shop, and half the village 'ud be there to give 'un a send-off.' On the stroke of the hour the master would come out with 'a girt roll o' one-pound notes under his arm' which he handed to the waggoner to pay for the groceries, stuffs, and clothing that were to be brought back. The Master himself used to ride to London on horseback, starting the following morning and arriving about the same time as the waggon. He would remain two days, selling and buying, and reach home again the end of the week. All Saturday evening, and up to the time of Morning Service on Sunday morning, the shop would be crowded with country folk, bartering eggs, butter, poultry and rabbits for commodities from town. When the bells ceased, the place was cleared, the shutters were put up, and the owner, after arraying himself in his Sunday best, would stalk down the street, his great prayer book under his arm, and enter the sacred building as the psalms were about to begin.

(*Islands of the Vale* by Eleanor Hayden)

9

Sheep, markets and transport by river

During the nineteenth century the Berkshire Downs marked the centre of one of England's greatest sheep-rearing areas. Scattered throughout the hills and in much of the Vale were numerous flocks of a whole variety of breeds. Lambourn, Chaddleworth, Childrey, Ashbury and Uffington prided themselves on their horned and Wiltshire sheep. At East Ilsley one farmer, a Mr. Stevens, selectively bred large animals, using a basic Southdown-Leicester cross and weeding out the smaller sheep. Fyfield, Harwell, Kingston Bagpuize, Abingdon, Wantage, Radley, Wytham, East Hendred and Cumnor maintained the native Berkshire breed, but Brightwell and the Moretons crossed Berkshire ewes with Southdown rams. The Wiltshire breed was favoured in flocks at Wallingford, Denchworth, Chaddleworth and Sparsholt. [1]

Although much crossed, the Berkshire breed was characterised by black faces, Roman noses, black or mottled legs and long tails.[2] Mr. Justice of Sutton Courtenay described the peculiar qualities of the Berkshire nott . . . "to be its great size, height on its legs, and weight when fatted . . . this variety of sheep is well calculated for the strong low-lands of this country." They seem "adapted to the low and cold lands, as they are proved to be more hardy for the fold; to fat sooner, and to be less liable to injury" than the horned or Wiltshire breed. [3]

1 Mavor pp.387-390.
2 Ibid p.381.
3 Ibid pp.381-2.

47

Quite naturally this emphasis on sheep farming had important implications upon industry and trade in the Berkshire towns, and in most centres one or more of the year's fairs specialised in the staple products of the region. The August Fair at East Ilsley was known far outside Berkshire's borders for its sheep and frequently there were up to 30,000 animals for sale at that time of year. In addition the Wednesday market dealt exclusively in sheep, and at Eastertide sheep markets took place twice a week for over a month. Ilsley was indeed thriving — so much so that one contemporary commented that the twisting hill which was the main street was throughout the year lined with stationary pens to hold the animals. The towns also dealt in wool and meat. Dorchester wool fair was established early in the nineteenth century and about 1810 the average price of wool was half-a-crown (12½p) a pound. Lambs at Michaelmas fair normally fetched £1 or twenty-five shillings (£1.25) each. In Abingdon today's Square by the war memorial was commonly called the Sheep Market, and fleeces were sold and meat dressed before local sale or transport up to London, and here from 1840 a specific wool fair was started.

Edward Loveden kept Leicester and Cotswold sheep; a record of his fleece output shows doubled output and rising income from wool production in the early years of the century. In 1801 his sheep yielded 261 fleeces, sold for £79 8s 6d (79.42½), while in 1806 he marketed 403 fleeces for £136 19s (£136.95).[4]

There was an attempt by the *Berkshire Agricultural Society* to establish a wool fair at Ilsley, but for a variety of reasons it was dropped. However the society eventually decided to split the event between Wantage and Newbury. So far as Wantage is concerned, the only reference I have found to a specific wool fair is in Jackson's Oxford Journal for July 27 1822 reporting the sale of over five thousand tods at 26s (£1.30) to 30s (£1.50) a tod. Possibly it was merged with the March Horse Fair or perhaps the May Fair, which

4   Ibid p.387.

traded particularly in cheese (a staple of the Vale), horses, clothes, and various manufactured goods.

At the weekly markets all kinds of products were offered for sale. From Stanford-in-the-Vale came cheeses made in the shape of a hare lying in its form and covered with chopped sage. Rabbit skins frequently appeared at Abingdon Market, for George Elwes at Marcham Park kept his own rabbit warren always very well stocked. Often he could sell them for 2s (10p) a pair. At Challow Mr. Exuperius Turner kept and bred tame white rabbits, making a small fortune from them. Mostly he sold them for fur trimmings, but those which did not find their way to London usually appeared at Wantage or Faringdon markets.

Market day at Wallingford was Friday, a day of hustle and bustle, when a corn market was regularly pitched beneath the pillars of the town hall. All manner of stalls were set up in the square, and over to one side pigs, sheep, cattle and chickens, divided off in wooden pens, came under the hammer of the local auctioneer.

The essentially local nature of trade early in the nineteenth century begs one vital question concerning transport. There were two links between north Berkshire and the capital: firstly came the age-old channel of trade, the Thames, and to supplement it some valuable and perishable commodities were moved by road waggon. One-hundred-ton barges reached Oxford and Abingdon from London, one-hundred-and-forty ton barges came to Wallingford, and seventy tons went further upstream to Lechlade where the river joined the Thames and Severn Canal. From Oxford, Abingdon and Wallingford the barge journey to London's wharves took four or five days according to the state of the water, while returning against the current took seven to ten days. It was the heavy, bulky, or low-cost goods which travelled by river — such commodities as malt for the London brewhouses, grain to be sold at Mark Lane, apples, timber, manufactured goods, coal, building stone, and fodder for sale in Whitechapel and Haymarket. Perishable or highly-valued articles such as groceries, meat, fruit, milk, and occasionally grain, were moved by road, and the waggons pulled by a team of horses (which could be seen on many a Berkshire highway) took just thirty hours for the journey, using the new roads built in short lengths by the Turnpike Trusts.

Throughout north Berkshire and parts of Oxfordshire the influence of waterways was keenly felt early in the nineteenth century, especially associated with coal movement. The Thames effectively joined the area to London, permitting Tyne coal to be brought up from the Coal Exchange to the riverside towns. By Thames barge goods could be sent to London and Oxford from the Wallingford wharf of Charles Morrell and from Abingdon to London at weekly intervals by Keats' Barges, which delivered goods to Brooks' wharf on Upper Thames Street in the City. The Bath and Bristol trade was handled each week by Messrs. Hopkins' barges from the Wilts & Berks canal wharf.[5] The Thames and Severn canal (1789) connected to South Wales, both the Wilts and Berks canal (1810) and the Kennet and Avon (1810) to Somerset's coalfield at Radstock, while the Oxford canal (1790) eventually linked with Staffordshire and the Midlands. The consequence of all this was that the average price of coal in north Berkshire was remarkably constant at about 30s (£1.50) a ton, and coal prices were kept low because nowhere in the county was more than a dozen miles from a waterway.

Plenty of alternative fuels existed for those people who could not afford coal; bean stubble was cut and commonly used in the western Vale, while old tan from Mr. Paul Sylvester's Wantage tanning yard was frequently burnt with underwood and faggots. For the really hard-pressed cottager, turf and peat would suffice to raise a fire, and in most of the Berkshire towns peat could be bought for a mere 13s (65p) a load, or 1s 6d (7½p) a bushel. As a load would cover most family requirements for nearly a year, it was much cheaper, though less efficient, than coal.[6]

5 PD 1823.
6 See p.24 for description of peat digging.

AMALGAMATION OF ABINGDON BREWERIES

Messrs. Morland & Co., Limited, in 1887 took over the business of John Thornhill Morland and Edward Morland of the Abbey and Eagle Breweries at Abingdon, and the business of Edward Henry Morland of the West Ilsley Brewery. They also acquired the breweries of Saxby & Co. of Abingdon and of Field & Sons of Shillingford. The Ilsley Brewery had been in the possession of the Morland family for many generations, John Morland having purchased the property from Benjamin Smith in 1711, and it is described as 'including the Malt House'. Allusion has already been made to the Abbey Brewery, which was formerly carried on by the Spenlove family and previous to them by the Child family. The old abbey buildings were used for the business. The Belcher family formerly held the Eagle Brewery, which is now the headquarters of the present firm of Morland & Co. Most of the buildings are old, and include the quaint early eighteenth century malthouse, as well as the new malthouse erected in 1904.

(The Victoria County History of Berkshire)

10

Sacking, leather and beer

In the early decades of the nineteenth century the north Berkshire market towns lost some of that glitter and zest which the prosperity of the cloth and sacking industry had in earlier decades brought to them. Gone were the days when Abingdon's chief sacking manufacturer, Thomas Westbrook, produced well over eight thousand yards of coarse cloth a week. Fast disappearing too were the factories at Wallingford and Wantage, once closely linked with the sacking and coarse cloth trade. But this is not to paint a picture of rapid commercial decay. As industries declined new ventures took their place and even more remained intact, but as a result of changes the local economy generally came to rest at a fresh and lower level of prosperity.

For several years Thomas Westbrook made over three hundred pieces of sacking each week, all conforming to the standard twenty-four by threequarters of a yard. However, by 1806 only seven hundred pieces were produced in the whole town, the decline having been largely caused by the removal of government contracts, and for some time it resulted in acute hardship for many Abingdon people. Nevertheless three thousand workers were still regularly employed in the Abingdon area and, from supplying the government, the master manufacturers turned their attention to making sail cloth for the Navy, hop pocketing for brewers, and sacks for the profusion of local millers. Rush and twine matting was a new business which had entered the town, and by 1806 considerable quantities were sold throughout southern England.

These mats, two dozen yards long, sold at a guinea a time and were widely adapted for halls, stairs, and passages in homes of the poor.

A fresh contract for biscuit bagging at the century's turn gave additional employment to one hundred and fifty people. In the hastily-converted bagging works men could earn 18s (90p) to £1 a week, but women only 5s (25p) and children 2s (10p). The reason for this was that sacking manufacture was pursued only partly in the town's factories. Much of it existed on a putting-our or domestic basis, whereby individual housewives worked on sacking in their own homes, the finished articles being collected regularly by a journeyman. Their pay was consequently much lower than in the factory, and perhaps this is a sound commentary upon industrial and social developments of the era.

At Wantage the situation seemed brighter. Around 1800 there was an emphasis on making quality sacking for army and naval hammocks, and this concentration on fairly high quality rather than the cheaper goods, as at Abingdon, may have prevented the decline in trade being so marked. By 1806 ten masters were established in sack making; flax and hemp were grown quite widely in the Vale of the White Horse, although initially largely for cattle feed and making oil cake, but later for weaving and rope making. Five of the manufacturers concentrated on a white cloth, sometimes called foulweather and used by workpeople. Ample water in the Letcombe brook was very well suited to fulling, the process of washing the semi-finished cloth.

Despite the importance of cloth making in Wantage, the chief emphasis at this period seems to have been upon tanning, and Paul Sylvester's tan yard, extending north of the market place between Grove Street and Garston Lane, was reputed to have been one of the biggest in England. Tanning here was expensive but the processes were of the most modern. Assisted by a German named Desmond, Paul Sylvester had hides fit for use in half the time other establishments took. Apart from a greater turnover in trade Sylvester experimented with various local types of bark, but always found that oak gave the best and greatest quantity of tanning. As a result considerable attention was given to oak cultivation and bark culture in several parts of north Berkshire, but perhaps too much money went into research for the venture was bankrupt by 1811.[1]

In a country area where pig raising was a speciality, bacon-curing was quite naturally widely followed in the market towns and each year many animals were slaughtered in Wantage and Wallingford, which both produced high quality bacon. But no place in the county could compete with Faringdon, for here the bacon houses of Edward Loveden were especially busy at Michaelmas and in April, and in all treated over eight thousand sides each year.

Wallingford too had its bacon-curing houses, but in comparison with Faringdon's they were insignificant. However, when one considers Wallingford's malt houses and breweries one realises immediately that here was an activity which was far from insignificant in the town's economy. There were eighteen malt houses scattered through the town; they all traded on the Thames by barge with London, and with Mr. Edward Wells' Wallingford Brewery, which was one of southern England's largest. The malt kilns produced brown malt, which had been dried with Chiltern beech wood, and pale malt, dried with coke and cinders. Wells' Brewery used each week some one hundred and twenty quarters of malt and was made into beer and porter for consumption in the numerous village inns throughout north Berkshire. Over at Abingdon several breweries operated, but Mr. Child's brew house alone produced a good quality porter — a beer which was originally made for market porters and labourers — it being dark in colour, bitter in taste, and brewed from partly charred malt.

About 1830 malting was important at Wantage, with the Day and Willoughby families being pre-eminent in the process, but the malt was used largely in individual households for they brewed their own beer. But there were

1 See p.35.
2 Mavor p.467.

55

two small brew houses in the town, one sited in an old inn called Thatchells in Church Street which was the forerunner of the Wantage Brewery, the other being Rockwell's Wantage Brewery. So far as local brews were concerned, beer was made at Lockinge during feast week, and villagers advertised their brews by hanging boughs above their door. Village breweries existed at Harwell, Ashbury, East and West Ilsley, Buckland and Lambourn. Although sacking and cloth-making may have been on the decline, the association of so many inns in the Berkshire countryside, barley growing in the Vale of the White Horse, and occasionally hop gardens on suitable soils, not only combined to make the area an important centre in the brewing business, but gave its economy a stability that was much needed during those uncertain decades.

FIRE

1884   *Royal Exchange*

Aug 7th. County Office, Abingdon.
For fire at Steventon

	£		
Use of Engine	*2*	*2*	*0*
Engineer		*12*	*0*
9 Firemen, 8 hours	*2*	*10*	*0*
24 pumpers, 5 hours	*3*	*10*	*0*
First informer		*2*	*6*
Men & firemen	*1*	*18*	*10*
Paid Horse Hire	*2*	*0*	*0*
	£12	*15*	*4*

Paid May 13/85
J. P. Whitehorn

56

11

Fairs, carriers, inns and banks

The White Horse Vale in the second and third quarters of the nineteenth century had a business and commercial life a whole world apart from that which exists today. Then, as now, Abingdon, Faringdon, Wallingford, and Wantage were the main market towns in the region, but there the similarity ends, for at that time they served a wholly agricultural area, and there were, too, smaller villages which had marketing functions but have now declined from their earlier prosperous condition — such places as East Ilsley, Sutton Courtenay, Shrivenham, Stanford-in-the-Vale, and Blewbury.

Commercial life centred in the towns, and it was here that the fairs and markets took place.[1] Wantage market was held on Saturdays when meat, poultry, butter, cheese and vegetables were offered for sale. But from 1845 a sample corn market was pitched each Wednesday, and although the Saturday market continued to flourish, the mid-week occasion gradually came to be the day when farmers met to strike bargains and to chat over the state of agriculture.

Each year Wantage had four fairs; the two-day Statute hiring fair half-way through October was the most important. Among the throng of hearty labourers would be scattered the carters and waggoners, with whipcord twisted round their hats; the thatchers wearing a fragment of woven straw; shepherds holding their sheep-crooks in their hands. Thus the job required was known to the hirers at a glance. A considerable trade was transacted in cheese, hops, domestic utensils, foodstuffs, furniture, and cheap clothing. The two hiring fairs at East Ilsley, one in mid-September and the second in mid-October, were largely for shepherds,

1 See tables 3, 4 & 5.

57

while the Wallingford fair at the end of September was mainly for carters and waggoners, with only a scattering of shepherds.

A whole wealth of other fairs took place. East Ilsley had sheep fairs established in the reign of Henry III which were nationally well-known. The annual series of markets and fairs started two weeks before Easter and ran through on alternate Wednesdays until July. On the first Wednesday in July came the wool fair, and the great sheep fairs followed on August 1 and 26, with anything up to fifty-thousand sheep being present. Shepherds who came to the fairs often started from home several days or a whole week before the event, driving their charges ten or a dozen miles along the Downland tracks and then resting. Often a pony and waggon would accompany the flock to take care of any ill or lame animals. The shepherd himself followed behind with his kit strapped on his shoulders over his smock, and his dogs close by. As the multitudes converged on the fair the individual flocks became an indistinguishable mass.

Besides the great event at Ilsley, Wantage had a cherry fair associated with nearby orchards, in mid-July, and a cattle and cheese fair in early March. The May Fair dealt in horses and cheese, the latter being a staple cottage product of the vale. Wallingford's cattle fair occurred in Easter week but was declining in the nineteenth century.

Abingdon maintained seven fairs a year. At the Lent Fair a large business was completed in horses, cattle and sheep. Stalls, for selling grain by sample and cottage produce, were set up. The Bull Fair, known also as Lombard Street Fair, was held in May and traded in horses, cows, sheep, bulls and cheese. Cottagers' stalls offered butter, farm cheese, cloth and baskets. Some business in horses and cattle took place at the June Ock Street Fair, but this was largely a pleasure fair. St. James' Fair in August did increasing trade in lamb's wool. Horses, sheep, fat cattle, store cattle and cheese were traded at the September Fair. Primarily for hiring servants, the Michaelmas Statute Fair was increasingly an entertainment and pleasure fair.

One report of this fair in the first decade of the

nineteenth century stated that dairy maids were hired at unusually poor wages, due primarily to the reduced price for Berkshire cheese. Those girls could expect only between five and ten guineas a year. Shepherds, for much longer hours, received £10 a year, while the carter took home £12 and his assistant, the under-carter, about £5. If one examines payments on a weekly basis a more vivid picture of wages can be constructed, for a day labourer was generally paid between 9s (45p) and 12s (60p), boys had 2s (10p), while women, mainly employed in summer and autumn, earned 3s (15p) or 4s (20p).[2] The report concluded that taskers (carters, ploughmen, shepherds) went off briskly and at high prices, the farmers being in a hurry to get their corn thrashed out for market.

Abingdon's final fair came in December, largely for cattle, horses and sheep. One year "a prodigious number of fine in-calf heifers of the Lancashire and Leicestershire breed" sold very briskly. "Fat sheep were also plentiful, but being held up at high prices by the graziers, they had a dull fair, and the sheep were chiefly driven home again."[3]

Faringdon had four fairs: for horses and cattle in February; a horse and pleasure fair at Whit; a Statute hiring fair of considerable size in mid-October; and a run-away fair at which servants who had already left employment settled at the hiring fair ten days earlier could be re-hired by new employers.

Having a close connection with these markets and fairs were the village carriers, who often rendered valuable services by running errands from the villages to the town. They could probably be seen in many a country lane, or waiting at an isolated toll gate for the keeper to let them through. Often they plied their business in one of those ornamental spring waggons, brightly painted, covered by a canvas awning, and pulled by one or maybe two horses. The waggon itself on the return journey would be piled high with household goods, furniture, parcels and sometimes even livestock.

2 JOJ
3 Ibid.

The country carrier would use an inn as his base. Benjamin Dunsdon plied between West Hanney and the Oxford Arms in Abingdon on Monday and Friday, while Henry Lloyd travelled the same route on Monday and Thursday of each week. The Charney Bassett carrier drew in at the Cock and Bottle, while the two men from Benson visited the Fighting Cocks and the King's Head. From Wantage Mr. Sims journeyed to Abingdon on Mondays and into Oxford on Wednesdays and Saturdays. Mr. Green from Blewbury visited the Crown Inn at Wantage, Mary Morning from Uffington arrived on Saturdays at the Red Lion, and Mr. Verney from Stanford-in-the-Vale was seen twice a week at the Bear, the Wantage Posting House. Also at Wantage on Saturdays Mr. Clack travelled in from Goosey to the Red Lion. Most days East Hanney's carrier, Mr. Herman, frequented the Blue Boar in Newbury Street. From his private house down Grove Street Mr. S. Sims's covered cart left twice each day to meet the up and down Parliamentary trains at Wantage Road Station, while Arthur Wells every Monday and Thursday connected Wantage and the scattered downland villages with Newbury.[4]

Edward Farley, a big-boned, robust countryman, was very well known at the Broad Face in Reading High Street; twice a day at noon and 8 pm he left with commissions for Shiplake. Wokingham was linked to Reading by two carriers; David Goodwin departed from Peach Street daily at 9 am for Reading's Saracen's Head, and John Gwyn plied between the towns three times a week. Bradfield's James Dodd called at the Rising Sun in Castle Street and James George the Black Boy in George Street, each twice a week. Bucklebury had four carriers travelling into Reading, Basildon had three, and Hampstead Norris two; Thomas Ferrebee, who was also a beer retailer, and William Pike the village brewer and grocer.

Similarly Wallingford was linked to its surrounding villages by a regular service of carriers. In from East Hagbourne came Benjamin Bosley promptly at 9 am each Friday. On market day Daniel Butler could be seen having come over from Upton, and James Lane from Aston

4 Kellys Directory 1860.

60

Upthorpe. Out to the Oxfordshire villages rode John Gray of Chalgrove, John Brown to Dorchester and Brian Saunders to Warborough; they all formed part of a fairly effective system of rural commercial communications.

Long distance carriers functioned regularly, but usually on the waterways. Henry Yeates on the Thames wharf (St. Helen's) dispatched goods each week from Abingdon to London and received orders from the metropolis, while goods from Bath and Bristol went quickly in Mr. J. Hoskins' boats from the foot of Mill Street in Wantage, along the Wiltshire and Berkshire canal.

All the country villages were connected to the local town by these carriers and the number of them and the frequency of their visits indicate the relative status of the towns. Oxford apart, Abingdon was by far the most important north Berkshire commercial centre, being closely followed by Wantage.

The number of inns a town had was an added criterion of its social and commercial standing, and here again Abingdon led the region. In 1862 there were no less than thirty-eight inns in the borough, with nine of them in Ock Street.[5] Over a century many inns have vanished; gone too are some of their curious names: there was the Red Cow in Bath Street, the Happy Dick stood opposite the Cock and Tree in Ock Street, the Fighting Cocks and the Cock Pit provided amusement as well as ale, and a house named the Two Brewers stood in Stert Street.

Wantage, too, had its share of inns, and a whole host of them clustered in the narrow lanes near the Market Place, but here too many have vanished. Inns like the Brandy Butt in Church Street, and the Jolly Waterman down on the wharf, the Globe Inn and the White Horse in Newbury Street have all gone. Looking out on to the Market Place were the Bell, the Shears, the Crown, the Alfred's Head, the Bear and the Falcon. Richard Bailey kept the Bear, which also served as the town's excise office and posting house; at the Falcon just over the way Stephen Blandy was landlord.

5   Ibid.

Wallingford, in common with other Vale towns, had a wealth of inns. John Allum kept the Two Brewers in Hart Street, Hannah and George Lovelock were joint landlords at the Mermaid near the town hall, while the Lamb Inn, described as 'a good inn of the old fashioned type' was Wallingford's posting house and the place where 'Oxfordshire and Berkshire farmers met' presumably at market and fair time. In all there were twenty-nine inns including a scattering with somewhat unusual names such as the Fat Ox, the Jolly Gardener in Wood Street, and Gerald's Hall, while in Fish Street Henry Wheeler kept the Green Tree.

At that time innkeepers often combined their alehouse with some other business. For instance, Benjamin Dorn of the Globe in Wantage was a rope and mat dealer, while William Simms at the Bell Inn dealt in coal and fish. Sam Markwell was by day a blacksmith and by night landlord of the Golden Fleece. Humphrey Enoch at Abingdon's Happy Dick sold matting and twine, and in his spare time made ropes.

During the third quarter of the nineteenth century the financial superiority of Abingdon is clear. Although only two banks existed, the London and County Bank which opened from 10 am to 3 pm with an extension to 5 pm on market days, and the Savings Bank, opening for an hour after midday only on Mondays, there were twenty-five insurance offices and agencies scattered throughout the town, far more than in any other north Berkshire town. At Wantage banking services were provided by the London and County Bank which maintained a branch of its Abingdon office in Newbury Street; it opened from 10 am to 3 pm every day with an extension to 5 pm on market day. A small Savings Bank operated from the town hall, being administered by Edward Ormond between noon and 1 pm on Wednesdays.

Mr. Ormond was one of Wantage's pair of solicitors; consequently he carried a considerable burden of public duties. Beside managing the Savings Bank, he was clerk to the magistrates, the petty sessions for the town and neighbourhood, meeting in the town hall on alternate

Wednesdays. He was also clerk to the guardians and to the commissioners of the Besselsleigh Turnpike Trust. The second town solicitor, William Dowdell Wasborough, kept his office in Newbury Street, and besides carrying on normal business, was coroner, registrar to the county court, clerk to the commissioners of taxes and agent for the Royal Exchange Assurance.

Other Wantage public officers included Benjamin Millard, superintendent of police in Mill Street; Mr. Edwards, who supervised the excise office in the Bear; and Mr. and Mrs. Knight who were master and matron respectively at Wantage Union Workhouse on Red House Hill, which at this time served thirty-four parishes with 17,308 people. Wantage itself according to the 1861 census had only 3,064 souls within its boundary.

THE HAZARDS OF COACH TRAVEL

The Southampton coach from Oxford, on Wednesday last, was enclosed so fast in the snow at Gore Hill, between this town and Ilsley, that the coachmen and passengers were necessitated to leave it. There is reason to fear that the coach from Southampton, on the same day, met with a similar fate, as it has not yet made its appearance.

(*Jackson's Oxford Journal*, January 23rd 1830)

The Stroud mail was overturned twice on Monday night last, owing to the density of the fog. No person was injured except the coachman, who was slightly bruised. The coach was eight hours behind time on passing through this town; the mail had been forwarded by a post chaise long previously.

(*Jackson's Oxford Journal*, December 31st 1831)

12

Manufacturers, tradesmen, letter carriers and coaches

Manufacturing which took place in the towns during the third and fourth quarters of the nineteenth century in many respects faithfully reflected the agricultural basis of the Vale economy. If one compares enterprise in this period with that of the 1820's, manufacturing had undergone a distinct structural change, and in some cases had suffered decline. But at Abingdon the beer trade still kept in business four malsters, three coopers and three brewers, along with no less than fifty alehouses. The town boasted twenty sacking makers, two carpet and rug manufacturers, and four black-smiths and white-smiths. The white smith worked 'white iron' or tin and also finished and polished metal goods as distinct from forging them;[1] I suppose there was very little difference between the white smith and Henry Rose, the tinman and brazier, whom we met in Wantage's Newbury Street.[2] In 1850 brewing and allied trades, along with cheap clothing manufacture, dominated the Abingdon industrial scene; at this time it was Berkshire's county town and kept in business several hop merchants, seven malsters, three coopers, and one brew house, namely the Eagle Brewery of E. H. Morland. In addition there were twelve rope, sack and matting makers all concentrated into Ock Street, twelve bakehouses and an iron and brass founder in Stert Street. In Bath Street were a couple of Berlin Repositories kept, one by a Mrs. Dean and the other by Mrs. Emmens; they began business as warehouses for special kinds of fine dyed woollens produced in Berlin and

1 PD 1823.
2 See p.67

used for knitting and tapestries but by 1860 had come to be woollen and fancy-goods shops. The two Italian Repositories formerly kept silk cloth used for linings and sometimes fruit, groceries and olive oil. Abingdon also had a couple of dyers, a fellmonger (a person who treated skins), a stay maker, several marine storekeepers, and three straw bonnet makers.

Industrial undertakings had various forms. The skilled man who worked at home, or in a small workshop nearby, was still very common. He might employ an apprentice and a couple of journeymen and may have put out work to other small-scale manufacturers in the same trade. His business was normally in goods which demanded close attention to detail but the mass-produced trades were rapidly developing beside the artisan.

Wallingford had its share of manufacturers and tradesmen. The shoe-makers and boot-makers — and in 1865 there were no less than fourteen of them — did excellent trade, especially Thomas Gill, an old-established firm in High Street. Along the lanes leading from the square down to the river one could count two straw-bonnet makers, a hatter, a couple of iron and brass founders, two wheelwrights — John Jennings of Castle Street and William Jennings whose yard was in Fish Street. Elsewhere varying numbers of coachbuilders, coopers, fellmongers and blacksmiths carried on their trades.

At this period the chief industry was brewing and malting, but there was also a considerable trade in salt; the two main salt dealers were Ben Bartram, who operated from the Oxford canal wharf, and W. B. & J. Hilliard, who kept storeyards near the Lower wharf by the railway station. Salt from Cheshire was moved through the canals of the Midlands, then down the Oxford canal and river Thames for distribution through the eastern Vale by these two Wallingford businesses. Similarly, coal used the canals and river, but increasingly was moved by rail. No less than five corn dealers shared Wallingford's trade, and grain not sold locally or to brewers usually reached London by river, road, and increasingly by railway in the 1860's.

1

2

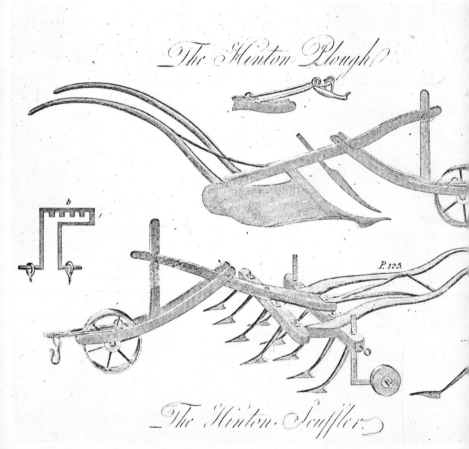

The Hinton Plough

b

P. 125

The Hinton Scuffler

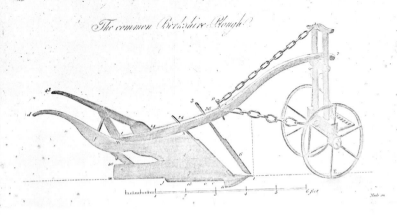

The common Berkshire Plough.

5

The Norfolk Plough.
recommended to be used on the light Soils of Berkshire.

6

The Suffolk Iron Plough.
recommended to be used on the heavy Soils of Berkshire.

7

Berks.

Hand Threshers at Work.

8

9

THRESHING BY MACHINERY.

10

11

A CHANNEL OF THE THAMES NEAR ABINGDON.

12

13

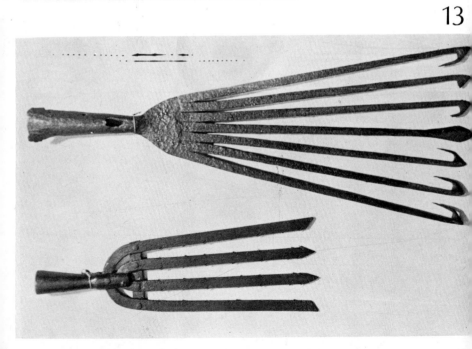

14

16

17

18

19

20

21

22

Berks.

Berkshire Nott Wether.)

23

26

27

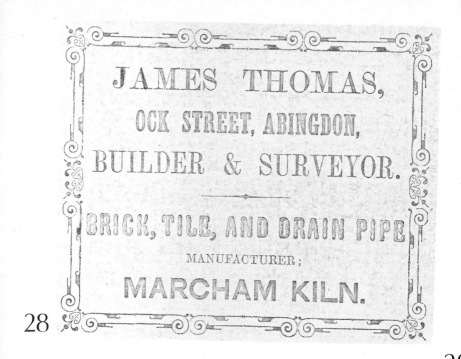

JAMES THOMAS,
OCK STREET, ABINGDON,
BUILDER & SURVEYOR.

BRICK, TILE, AND DRAIN PIPE
MANUFACTURER;
MARCHAM KILN.

30

31

32

Wantage too, had a similar variety of artisans and manufacturers. Sacking and hemp goods were still made, but had declined in importance by 1860. Taking their place in the economy of the town were two flourishing engineering works which made some of the agricultural implements which were increasingly in demand on the farms in these days of improvement and mechanisation. The White Horse Foundry made steam engines, threshing machines, and such agricultural implements as the Berkshire plough, harrows, drills, and so forth. The Nalder works, just out of Wantage at East Challow, were for general agricultural engineering and foundry work but they too soon entered into the machine-making business.[3] Numerous other trades were followed in Vale towns and villages, many being totally characteristic of the later nineteenth century. At Wantage, Henry Pulley made hats, William Liddiard was the auctioneer and bone merchant. In his yard off Wallingford Street he made artificial fertiliser from bones. Grove Street contained the premises of a varied selection of traders; George Ball made boots and shoes. Thomas Barnard was a furniture broker and fruiterer, Richard Barton a smith and farrier, and Henry Rose, tinman and brazier. Newbury Street held two 'dame' schools, one run by Miss Bugbird and the other by Miss Anne Dynham. Both were advertised as Ladies' Boarding Schools, while down Mill Street James Belcher combined his mixed boarding and day school with a small printing works.

Recalling the area's association with pig rearing, it is not surprising to find pork butchery businesses in every local market town. At Wantage, Richard Dixon had such a pork shop, and his brothers, John and William, were both hay and corn dealers, one in Mill Street, the second in Wallingford Street. William Redwood kept the neighbourhood's sole sieve and basket making workshop in Mill Street; Mrs Elizabeth Lewis was a glove maker in Newbury Street, while on the same small premises, George Lewis ran a china, glass and Birmingham warehouse.

3 WHC p.91.

Manufacture of bricks, tiles, drainpipes and chimney pots was an expanding activity in the Vale. There were brickworks at Chawley (Cumnor), Drayton, Marcham, East Challow, Culham, Farnborough and Childrey. Outside the area a major enterprise was situated at Tilehurst (Reading), and there were at least twenty-two brickworks in the Newbury vicinity including four at Hermitage, five in the Newbury town area, two at Kintbury and one each at Beedon, Wickham, Hampstead Norris, Upper Basildon, Frilsham, Cold Ash, Donnington, Midgham and Thatcham. Urban expansion increased demand for building materials and Childrey brickworks was ideally situated beside the Wilts & Berks canal (as were East Challow kilns) enabling easy transport to expanding Bristol and Swindon. Much building material, however, was used locally and examples can still be seen in virtually every Vale village. These kilns made dull-red bricks, also grey and blue-black glazed-bricks which when set in patterns of red brick had the effect of varying the facades of buildings; they were frequently used as headers in vertical stripes between windows, while later in the century and especially in the Wantage area whole walls were built from them. To see this builder's device to its best advantage look at the Georgian facades around the south side of Wantage market place, at West Hanney House, at the Old Rectory in Farnborough or the barns attached to Abbey Farm, Goosey.

The normal process of brickmaking was to dig clay, then to mix it in a pug mill with water and sand. The bricks were shaped by mould, hand, or by extrusion, then often wire cut before drying in the open air. As space allowed they were put in the kilns for firing, then placed in stock. At Childrey there were three down-draft kilns, each probably capable of holding up to 12,000 bricks for a firing. The clay pit's outline is clear on the ground, two of the three kilns remain and the pug mill where bricks were shaped can be found.

In villages surrounding the market towns all kinds of artisans plied their trade, and each village was to a large degree self-sufficient, for in terms of the transport available at this period they were a considerable time and distance from their local town. There were abundant boot and shoe makers, for instance at Kingston Bagpuize and Sutton Courtenay (which each had two), at Marcham, Denchworth, Childrey, East Hanney and West Hanney. In 1850 the measure of self-sufficiency at East Hanney was in a pair of blacksmiths (William Cox and James Ashfield), a butcher (William Giles), wheelwright (Henry Godfrey), four shopkeepers, two millers (Thomas Patrick and H. A. Hall), baker (John Stevenson), malster (William Cook), corn dealer (Thomas Stevenson), pig dealer (John Johnson), fruiterer (Benjamin Hearman), boot and shoe maker (John Piggott) and three carriers (Benjamin Dunsden, Mary Hearman and Jonathan Hearman) who between them visited Abingdon, Wantage and Oxford at various times during the week to fetch those goods which the village folk could not provide for themselves. West Hanney had a similar range of tradesmen: three shopkeepers, a single carrier, a wheelwright (James Belcher), carpenter (Alfred Belcher), boot and shoe maker (Thomas Booker), baker (William Burson), fruiterer, and in Richard Lloyd a threefold function of butcher, beer retailer and grocery shopkeeper.

At Uffington there is a complete study of the tradesmen who worked there between 1847 and 1907. During that sixty-year period the village had nine bakers, one of them a woman, namely Mrs Imms, carrying on for a short time in 1887 a family tradition which extended back to 1854. John and Henry Packer were blacksmiths between 1877 and 1907, while both John and Stephen Jenkins also carried on that trade from 1854 down to 1904. There were two partnerships of brick and tile makers, and a whole host of carpenters (eleven), including three from the Briscoe family, eight dressmakers, four glaziers, six plumbers, four sawyers, eleven shoe and boot makers who included Mrs Kilpatrick carrying on her husband's trade for one year in 1898. The village also had four wheelwrights, two tailors and a single milliner, groom, farrier, horse trainer and jockey, all at a period when the village population fluctuated between 670 and 530 people.[4]

4   DDU 1847-1907.

As the village self-sufficiency broke down and the town hiring fairs decayed, the newspapers, with their increasing volume of advertisement, flourished. Whether one factor is related to the other is difficult to decide, but in 1860 the press flourished, for the *Abingdon Herald* foreshadowed *The North Berks Herald* series of today, while the *Reading Mercury* served Wallingford and the east of the county; additionally Wallingford had in Fish Street the offices of the *Berks and Oxon Advertiser*. At Faringdon the *Faringdon Free Press* was published by Jeremiah Smith, the man who also originated and manufactured the patent self-adhesive envelope. A rival of the *Free Press* was the smaller *Faringdon Advertiser* which Charles Luker published in London Street.

With improved road and rail communications Abingdon's postal service in the period 1850-75 appears to be efficient. Collections for Wantage and Faringdon were taken at 9.30 am; for the West of England at 9.35 pm; and for London at 10 pm. Each weekday there were four deliveries: for mail from local towns and London at 7 am; from the north at 9.30 am; a third delivery at 11.30 am: and a final one at 4.30 pm. Wantage had two collections and deliveries a day; in the morning the post box for mail to be delivered all over England closed at 10.40 am and the mail was despatched to Faringdon Road Station some twenty minutes later. The evening post closed at 9.15 pm and left for the station at 9.45 pm. Letters for the town and surrounding villages arrived at Faringdon Road at 3 am and 1.40 pm and were then sorted in Wantage before being delivered in the town or sent on to the villages.

Letter-carriers and messengers had given their services through much of the area since the previous century; although sometimes duplicating the tasks of the carriers, they were essentially separate. Mr Richard Wake took letters and notes along the road between Abingdon, Culham, Clifton and Burcot. John Porter plied through Marcham, Frilford and Garford. A messenger (as distinct from a letter carrier), named John James, journeyed daily to the villages on the route from Abingdon, through Harwell, to Chilton.

Early in the century's second quarter we learn a little about road-passenger transport from the Berkshire towns. In 1825 Abingdon was linked to London and neighbouring towns by seven distinct coach services usually carrying four people inside and between five and eleven people outside. To London *The True Briton* departed from the New Inn, Market Place, at 9 am three times a week and the *Light Coach* daily from Ock Street's Lamb Inn at 8 am. Oxford services began from the Red Lion in High Street and Rising Sun in Sheepmarket at 10 am each day, while *The Dart* took people to Reading from the New Inn daily at 3.30 pm. Southampton could be reached any weekday by leaving from the Lamb Inn at 9 am while twice a week the Red Lion saw a late afternoon coach depart for Wantage.

Faringdon, Wantage and Wallingford had similar services. *The Defiance* travelled from Highworth through Faringdon (Bell Inn 7 am), Wantage (Bear Inn), Wallingford, Reading and Maidenhead to London three days a week in each direction. *Royal Mail Coaches* daily connected Faringdon with Bristol and Oxford, through Abingdon. The Stroud coach to London left the Green Dragon at Faringdon on Tuesdays, Thursdays and Saturdays at 6 am and journeyed by way of Abingdon and Henley to the metropolis. Wallingford was on the Reading - Oxford coach route as well as the Highworth coach route to London. In addition a daily mid-afternoon coach — *Benoe's Conveyance* — departed for Reading from the Duke's Head. [5]

With the more reliable communications that had evolved by 1870, except possibly to the most distant villages, the countryside was becoming more dependent upon the towns. Nevertheless north Berkshire villages were still to a considerable degree self-sufficient. Kingston Bagpuize, with a population of less than three hundred supported a harnessmaker, a victualler (on Newbridge Wharf), a blacksmith, glazier, two shoe and bootmakers, a mason, tailor, wheelwright and a baker. The villages of West and East Hanney with a combined population of 498 people could still boast seven shops, a blacksmith, bootmaker, corn factor, baker, beer retailer, coal dealer, wheelwright,

5   PD 1823.

a bricklayer and two carriers, while Marcham had a brick and tile maker.

In addition every mill along the Letcombe and Childrey brooks and the River Ock was at a peak of prosperity; the paddle wheels had rarely turned so fast, and this despite the co-called great agricultural depression, caused by the massive import of American grain, which was about to break over rural England.

THE BERKSHIRE WAGGON

The Berkshire Waggon is generally admired for its peculiar lightness and elegance, and though it varies a little in its construction in different parts of the county, it combines the three great requisites; easy draught, strength, and a facility of being loaded and unloaded from its being low built.

(General Survey of the Agriculture of Berkshire
by William Mavor)

13

The country craftsmen

Almost all the rural crafts which were once so closely linked to agriculture in the Berkshire Vale have disappeared. We have seen already that through most of the nineteenth and early twentieth centuries every village and market town had a selection of craftsmen. The smiths, carpenters and wheel-wrights abounded, while here and there ladder-makers, hurdle-makers and basketmakers found these prosperous years.

All over the Vale were examples of crafts running in families. For instance, at Uffington John Jenkins was succeeded by Stephen Jenkins in 1893 as a village blacksmith, while at another forge worked John Mattingley (1854-63). Henry Packer ran his blacksmith's shop from 1877 to 1901 and was joined in 1892 by John Packer who continued the business. Similarly three of the Bridgeman family, Thomas, Esau and Cain, were Uffington bricklayers between 1878 and 1907. About 1855 Charles Cox ran the village smithy at East Hanney and William Cox worked the West Hanney forge. Also at that period James Belcher was Hanney's wheel-wright, serving the dozen farms in the villages and occasionally working for farmers in surrounding settlements.[1]

The wheel-wright's skilled job has now fallen on evil days owing to rapid substitution of motors and metal wheels for horse-drawn and oxen-drawn carts, but once no type of vehicle was too difficult for local craftsmen; all types of country carts were built and the glory of the craft was that four wheeler — the Berkshire waggon.

1   See DDU p.14.

Any Berkshire wheel-wright's shop held the usual carpenter's tools — bench, vices, sawing bench made from split logs with peg legs inserted. Then around the dusty walls were all kinds of tools peculiar to his trade. For instance at James Field's workshop in South Moreton were a variety of saws, gouges, chisels, gauges and numerous other small but essential tools, while Isaac Gearing at Milton and John Reckets at Kingston Bagpuize had more specialised tools — the spoke-dogs used for fitting wheel spokes and allowing the felloe or outside rim to be added. Over to one side would be the wheel horse — that four-legged frame which carried wheels undergoing repair, so that draw and spoke-shaves could conveniently be used upon them. Sometimes wheel-wrights turned their hand to ladder-making and in the workshop of Stephen Goddard and of James Wells, both at Brightwalton, could be seen a ladder-maker's horse, a bench which craftsmen sat astride while shaping, replacing or fitting ladder rungs. Around the side walls hung all manner of fierce-looking tools: augers, spoke planes, bark-strippers, beetles, calipers and dividers. Standing outside would often be several finished ladders, neatly painted and waiting collection or sale to some downland farmer. Other wheel-wrights traded at Steventon (John Gerring), Long Wittenham (Edmund Tame), Sutton Courtenay (John Neville), Marcham, Longworth, Faringdon (four), Uffington and Lambourn (two).[2]

In some ways the hurdle-maker's job was more specialised than either wheel-wright or ladder-maker, and his skill was frequently confined to the downland villages of north Berkshire. John Eagles was Brightwalton's hurdle-maker — right in the midst of Berkshire's premier sheep country, an area famed during many centuries for its wool; James Stanmore worked at East Ilsley and James Hamblin at Shefford.[3] Hurdles were essential for folding sheep on growing crops and, when dressed with straw, provided excellent wind breaks during the lambing season. Oak, chestnut, withy and ash were the usual woods and to split the lengths for hurdle heads and rails the craftsman

2 BD 1854.
3 Ibid.

used a freshly sharpened frommard. The brace and gouge drilled mortise holes while the draw knife shaped the cleft timber. Now and again one comes across a survival of this most ancient of crafts and a short while ago I found a hurdle-maker working in what seemed the most unlikely place, close to Day's Lock just below the church at Little Wittenham, with around the site a whole wealth of withy and, close at hand, abundant ash.

Even in the early nineteenth century one had to look more carefully in north Berkshire for a basket-maker than for the other craftsmen, but those who did carry on this trade could often trace it back to very early times, for it came to Britain two thousand years before Christ, and its pre-historic techniques have remained almost unchanged down to the present day. Five examples of basket-makers in north Berkshire have come to my notice, one at Faringdon and the others at Cholsey, Wantage and Abingdon. Down Faringdon's Marlborough Street, just above Scarcebrook the coach builder, was the basket-making workshop of William Lavington; over at Cholsey Ruben Lewis followed a similar trade; at Wantage William Redwood combined his business with sieve-making in Mill Street. In 1823 Abingdon had two basket-makers in Henry Brown and John Flory, while nearby worked three brush-makers — Joseph Lloyd, John Stanchard and Thomas Wiblin.[4] These craftsmen will have made the fruit pots to hold 50 lbs of plums which were used in large numbers in the Vale orchards; these have now been superseded by wooden boxes. Withy, flourishing on that low-lying ground subject to annual flooding around the Thames and in the Vale of the White Horse, was the ideal raw material for basket-makers. Seasoned bundles were first boiled to make them supple. Pot-makers then sorted canes into grades suitable for bottoms, upsetting, sides, borders and handles. Their first task each morning was to make sufficient bottoms to last the day; the average number was seven or eight pots per workman. Basket-makers near the Thames often made fish pots and now and again lengthy eel traps, but their main

4   PD 1823.

activity, especially in villages on the rich greensand belt, was in making fruit pots. Now, a century later, almost all trace of the once-plentiful basket-maker has gone from the countryside.

As at Abingdon, brush-making was elsewhere frequently combined with basket-making. At Reading five craftsmen made baskets and brushes while Charles Swain in Hosier Street specialised in brushes alone. [5]

Cabinet-makers, upholsterers, chair-makers, boat-builders, axle-spring makers, coach-builders, coopers, french polishers, gun-makers, patten and clog makers, saddlers and harness-makers abounded in Reading half-way through the nineteenth century.[6] Every town in the Vale had some of these crafts represented. Abingdon's Patten and Clog-maker was Charles Coxeter in Ock Street; four men ran coach-building enterprises; Thomas Barrett built boats off West St. Helen Street. Wallingford's pair of cabinet-makers looked across the Market Place and High Street to the coach-builder's yard, the leather-cutting workshop of Butcher & Son, and two of the town's four stonemasons' yards.[7] At Faringdon were two gunsmiths and at Wantage three watch-and-clock-makers.[8]

So far as clock-making was concerned, Berkshire had for long been well known for the craft. The eighteenth century produced as clock-makers John Lord at Faringdon, Edward Caudwell in Blewbury, a Mr. Bunce, who carried on a thriving business at Wantage, and William Gunn, who was equally prosperous and well known for his timepieces in Wallingford. By the nineteenth century Berkshire clock-makers had multiplied in number to some fifty-eight in the whole county and almost half of them were concentrated in the northern portion of Berkshire. For instance, in Abingdon there resided five different craftsmen. People by the name of Meyer, Payne, Pitt, Pond and Whitham, all of whom were thriving in the 1820's, had moved away from the skilled manufacture of specific clocks [9]

5   BD 1854.
6   Ibid.
7   Ibid.
8   Ibid.
9   BAJ Vol 30 pp.148-52.

to order, and were by now making a wide variety of standardised timepieces for a much-increased local demand.

At Faringdon, where craftsmen by the names of Monnoa, Kirkpatrick and Strauss worked, the situation had similarly changed to standardised clock-making. At the same time Lambourn saw the workmanship of Messrs. Hill and Thatcher; at Wallingford worked men by the name of Cross, Howes, Payne and Player; while Wantage produced as timepiece-makers a Mr. Allen and Mr. Belcher.

BALLAD OF THE SCOURING OF
THE WHITE HORSE

The owld White Horse wants zettin to rights,
And the Squire hev promised good cheer,
Zo we'll gee un a scrape to kip 'un in zhape,
And a'll last for many a year.

A was made a lang lang time ago
Wi a good dale o' labour and pains,
By King Alfred the Great when he spwiled their consate
And caddled ¹ they wosbirds ² the Danes.

The Bleawin Stwun in days gone by
Wur King Alfred's bugle harn,
And the tharnin tree you may plainly zee
As is called King Alfred's tharn.

There'll be backsword play, and climmin the powl,
And a race for a peg, and a cheese,
And us thenks as hisn's a dummel³zowl
As dwont care for zich spwoorts as theze.

---

1   to worry
2   a bird of woe, an evil omen
3   dull or stupid

78

14

Games, gaiety and gore

Looking back we may consider our great-grandfathers' partiality for bull-baiting and cock fighting, for pugilism or backswording to be barbaric and distasteful, but in towns and villages up and down the country these frequent occasions were times for celebration, days in the annual round to be eagerly awaited.

One great occasion in the Vale was the pastime accompanying the scouring of Uffington's White Horse. It usually took place in Uffington Castle but occasionally moved to Kingston Lisle or Seven Barrows Farm. All the villages and towns in the Vale claimed a part in the task of Scouring the Horse, and therefore in the revel which followed. The last scouring was in 1857, and the normal sporting events ensued, but in addition were a pig race across the hilltop, a race for a cheese rolled down the Manger, and a cart-horse race. Fortunately the record of this revel is preserved by Thomas Hughes, and earlier ones in correspondence between Francis Wise, of Oxford, and Dr. Mead, the antiquarian. [1]

The handbill ran as follows:-

PASTIME

To be held on the occasion of the Scouring of the White Horse, September 17th and 18th, 1857.

At a meeting held at the Craven Arms, Uffington, on the 20th day of August 1857, the following resolutions were passed unanimously:-

[1]   BB pp.137-152

79

First   *That a pastime be held on the White Horse Hill, on Thursday and Friday, the 17th and 18th of September, in accordance with the old custom at the time of "The Scouring of the Horse".*

2dly   *That E. Martin Atkins, Esq. of Kingston Lisle, be appointed Treasurer.*

3dly   *That prizes be awarded for the following game and sports. That is to say —*

Backsword	*Old gamesters*	*£8*
Play	*Young gamesters*	*£4*
Wrestling	*Old gamesters*	*£5*
	Young gamesters	*£4*

A Jingling match

Foot races

Hurdle races

Race of cart-horses in Thill harness (for a new set of harness)

Donkey race (for a flitch of bacon)

Climbing pole (for a leg of mutton)

Races down the Manger (for cheeses)

A pig will be turned out on the down, to be the prize of the man who catches him (under certain regulations); and further prizes will be awarded for other games and sports as the funds will allow.

4thly   *That no person be allowed to put up or use a stall or booth on the ground, without the previous sanction of Mr. Spackman, of Bridgecombe Farm (the occupier), who is hereby authorized to make terms with any person wishing to put up a stall or booth.*

Signed. E. MARTIN ATKINS, Chairman.

A contemporary account of the scouring of 1780 tells us that upwards of thirty-thousand people saw the pastime in that year, and the contests and prizes were especially noteworthy.[2] The winner of a three-mile pony-race had a silver cup, and cheeses were to be won by yokels who chased them as they rolled down the Manger. The women raced for smocks, while a side of bacon went to the victor in an asses' race. Further — something truly rural — five shillings was for the winner of a grinning match through a horse's collar. It would stretch the ingenuity even of a Berkshire man to judge this competition . . .

Far more serious were the contests demanding skill and strength, not forgetting an element of cunning. Here local reputations were at stake and the encounters attracted shepherds, carters and farmers' lads from far and wide. Wrestling took place for a pair of fine buckskin breeches, and cudgel-playing for a pair of silver buckles. On one occasion a wrestling champion fell into the Wilts and Berks canal, presumably semi-conscious, while homeward bound, and died there; a verdict of kicked at wrestling was returned on the poor man, while at another pastime Tim Gibbons, an Uffington fellow turned highwayman, rode up to win the backswording prize from the champion of the day. But no sooner had he trounced the man than he remounted and galloped off to avoid arrest.

These Uffington pastimes had something of a Bank Holiday spirit about them, but far more serious events took place at Market (East) Ilsley, where the occasion of the annual sheep fair coincided with the coursing meeting. Two hounds running a hare, the one working best being declared the winner — that is the theme of competitive coursing, but far more skill attaches to it than can be admitted in such a general description. The Berkshire Downs — wild, open and windswept — are ideal country for the sport and the Ilsley meeting was always a success. Accounts indicate that the 1826 affair attracted abnormally large crowds, "the dogs were in fine condition, the hares strong, and the sport consequently excellent.'[3] Right along the Downs from Ilsley

2   Reading Mercury May 22 1780.
3   JOJ 25 Nov 1814.

to Ashbury was noted ground for coursing, and meetings often took place above Ardington and Lockinge even to the turn of this century. One remarkable adherent to the sport lived and died at Compton Beauchamp. She wrote her own epitaph, telling of her attachment to the hounds and hare, and today it is on her tomb for all to read;

Reader, if ever sport to thee was dear
Drop on Ann Richards' tomb a tear.
Who when alive with piercing eye
Did many a timid hare descry.
At books she laughed; at Pope and Clarke,
And all her joy was Ashdown Park.
But Ann at length was spy'd by Death,
Who coursed and ran her out of breath.
No shifting, winding turn could save
Her active life from gaping grave."

Bull-baiting was certainly a far more bloody affair. Many a country market place and village green in north Berkshire saw these animals attacked by bulldogs. In those days people saw in it a useful purpose, and would never dream of killing an animal before it had been baited; it so improved the beef! By 1835 worrying bulls, bears, and dogs was illegal but Wantage had the invidious reputation of being one of Berkshire's last towns to comply with the law. People from all over the neighbourhood drove to witness the bait; crowds encircled the Market Place, the inns overflowed, and the back alleys swarmed with pickpockets. The bull, tethered by a long chain, was attacked by a bulldog who leapt at its nose. When the bull pitched the dog high into the air the crowd howled with delight; they enjoyed the fun! But when the dog bit its teeth into the bull's nose they shouted their disapproval as the sport was over and the animal despatched for slaughter. Good Friday was Berkshire's favourite bull-baiting day, but the well-recorded displays at Wokingham, a notorious town for baiting, always took place on St. Thomas' Day just before Christmas.[4]

Among other notable Berkshire sports one might include

4   BB pp.244-258.

prize fighting and this part of England was particularly favoured because London was so close. But often there were purely local fights. One such was at Kennington Feast in 1762 between a Mr. Earle and a man called Hen-Toe. The contest lasted for a full ten minutes and on one side of the Isis, but the over-eager crowds forced the contestants to cross the river, where they fought for twenty minutes more until Hen-Toe gave in.[5]

Some years later Kennington saw another contest, between an Oxford butcher and a Cowley carpenter, but on this occasion the fight was properly conducted and lasted for eight rounds, the butcher eventually being the winner.[6] It was after Abingdon races one year that a number of pitched battles took place on Culham Heath. A fight between a man from Hanney and one from Sutton Courtenay was a tremendous affair and went to fifty rounds in front of a crowd said to number thousands. The Sutton man finally won, confirming an earlier victory at Drayton over his Hanney opponent. But prize fights did not always turn out as expected. As a result of a battle for twenty guineas between a Witney man and a Weston-on-the-Green man at Newbridge, one contestant died and the other was hanged for wilful murder. But the most curious contest was at Cothill Feast in 1830 between one man six feet tall weighing fifteen stone, and the other measuring four feet two inches and weighing nine stone. "The science of the dwarf was more than a match for the strength of the giant; and, consequently, after forty-five minutes' hard fighting, the little un bore away the bays"[7]without having received any punishment. [8]

Competitive pigeon-shooting took place at Caldecott House, Abingdon, "for an enormous fat hog of almost forty score, as the prize, the possession of which had been twice contested by the cock-fighters of Abingdon and Oxford."[9]

5   JOJ 7 Aug 1762
6   JOJ 24 Jan 1824.
7   Bay leaves of the victor.
8   3 July 1830.
9   Ibid 17 April 1830.

From earliest times cock fighting seems to have found especial favour with Berkshire people, and matches between birds belonging to the farmers and gentlemen of surrounding counties took place frequently in the towns. The Crown Inn at Faringdon had a notorious pit, and one event occurred there in 1758 between the noblemen and gentlemen of Berkshire, Gloucestershire and Oxfordshire. While at the New Inn, Abingdon, twenty-five fights at two guineas a battle took place between the farmers of Oxfordshire and Berkshire. The event took three days to complete, and ran at the same time as Abingdon races. Inn names often furnish evidence of past sports, and Abingdon, like numerous other towns, once had its Cock Pit Inn. The remains of a village cockpit can be seen to this day at Long Wittenham close to the school gate and is still clearly marked by a saucer-shaped depression in the ground some thirty feet across. [10]

As with cock fighting so too with prize fighting; both took place at Abingdon concurrently with the March horse races, at a time when the town was alive with strangers. The race course on Culham Heath was used for several meetings a year before it was enclosed, and then racing was transferred to Abingdon Common on the Marcham Road. One famous horse was owned by an Abingdon innkeeper, and he came to buy it in a curious way. This Mr Alder surreptitiously spent money his wife gave him to pay the brewer on State lottery tickets, and with all the luck in the world he won £20,000 — purchasing with it a grey called Sulphur, which won the races of 1768. So good was the animal that it eventually passed to the Duke of Cumberland.

By 1804 the Abingdon Races were nationally known and horse sales were combined with the second day's events, while a few years later a race ball and dinner became an annual event in the County Hall. A later reliable account tells of Abingdon Races being considered equal to any meeting in the country, but now all has gone and Abingdon's horse racing tradition is lost.

10   WHC pp.133-4

Before the 1826 meeting two horses were taking customary exercise on the course, by name, Comedian and Trinculo, when an accident occurred, for "Comedian bolted and threw his rider, when Trinculo which is a very vicious animal, followed his example, and also threw his rider: both horses taking across the Common, arrived at the river Ock just above the Mill, when Comedian plunged in, and Trinculo followed; they were, however, with difficulty rescued from their situation. On the first day of the races Comedian won the cup and Trinculo the Abingdon Stakes.'[11]The 1835 meeting saw a new race — a hunter's stake of ten guineas for non-thoroughbreds, to be the property of a gentleman resident in Berkshire, Oxfordshire or Gloucestershire, and to have been at the kill of at least six foxes in the season.

Another occasion for merriment was the fair or village feast. Many local fairs have decayed, such as the great August Sheep Fair at East Ilsley which attracted people from far and wide. The Harwell Horse Fair has gone, but the fairs in the market towns have survived at Wantage, Faringdon, Abingdon and Wallingford, although they have evolved to serve a far different purpose than that of a century ago. Other fairs have become merged with village feasts and are still celebrated, but, like the Market Fairs in a much different form from the original.

Feasts in the Vale of the White Horse were not the usual Statute Feasts — we might call them Bank Holidays now — but feasts of the dedication of the church, and were first held in the churchyard to commemorate the day the church was opened, usually on the particular patron saint's day of the church; the feast was always held on that day for centuries following.

Uffington feast has been carefully described by Thomas Hughes. It took place in a field next to the church where all the cheapjacks, small-traders' stalls, and penny peep-shows had assembled. Hughes would have us believe that the peep-shows contained such things as pink-eyed ladies, boa-constrictors, dwarfs and wild Indians! But always the centre of attraction was the raised rough-plank stage where the wrestling and back-sword ing took place.[12]

11 JOJ 16 Sept 1826.
12 See *Tom Brown's School Days.*

Feast-time was an occasion when children made an effort to be at home if they had been working in the town, and they brought their wages and a present with them. It was the only time in the year when so many young men and women were seen going round the village, and like their elders dressed in best clothes; most households managed to have a bottle of homemade wine and a feast-cake on the table for all comers to partake of.[13] Descriptions of nineteenth century feasts tell of contemporary country dress. Men had clean white smocks or maybe velvet or fustian coats with brilliantly coloured waistcoats; the women always wore those long scarlet cloaks which were the proper outdoor dress for them. The garment often descended in the family from mother to daughter so great a value was put upon the cloak.

As at Uffington, feasts and revels elsewhere have died, for instance Challow feast which was held on Trinity Sunday, and the following day games took place. Locals raced for ducks in the Wiltshire and Berkshire canal, no doubt following the custom at Grove.[14] Now that the canal is disused the custom has disappeared. At Sutton Courtenay the feast and fair which was held at Corpus Christi has lapsed, along with St. Denys' feast at Stanford-in-the-Vale, where beside the usual sporting contests was held a competition for climbing the greasy pole. The old hands cunningly allowed the younger fellows to try their luck and when the grease had been sufficiently wiped, climbed the pole with ease and claimed the shoulder of mutton.

At Grove, Duck Races took place each year on the pinning-up night of the feast. A fair gathered on the green. In the waters of the Letcombe brook, specially dammed for the occasion, the races took place; ducks released half way between the two bridges which cross the stream were chased by the competitors. Usually the duck was quickly taken and became the property of the captor. A slightly different type of sport found Sparsholt as its centre during the second quarter of the nineteenth century, for the village made its name as a local and national centre for Archery, under the

13   WHC pp.67-68.
14   WHC p.102.

keen guidance of Colonel Hippisley of the Manor House. In 1831 he founded the West Berkshire Archery Club and instituted the York Round, consisting of seventy-two arrows at a hundred yards, forty-eight at eighty, and twenty-four at sixty. This club was limited to twelve members who met at one another's houses all over England in order to shoot the Round, and Thomas Hughes' father, John Hughes of Uffington, gave the village toxophilites a fine cup for annual competition.

But such a brief excursion into some of our forebears' sports and pastimes can do but scant justice to them. However, it may illustrate how willing they were to provide their own entertainment, often quite spontaneously. But so far as spontaneity is concerned, one must mention the Mummers, who at Christmas time came into action performing their time-worn play illustrating the final victory of good over evil, which they recited at houses in the local villages. The words at Drayton followed the traditional pattern, except that St. George became King George, a stranger and Merrian replaced Jack Vinny and Happy Jack. Characters in the Cholsey play included Doctor, Tipton Slasher, Father Beelzebub and Tom the Tinker, who introduced himself as being "no small beer drinker, I tell the landlord to his face, the chimney corner is my place". At Brightwell I had recited to me much of the village play; in the opening lines Molly sets the stage for the audience, all eagerly awaiting the performance:

"A room, a room, I do desire, for all my brave
    and gallant souls,
Stir up the fire and make a light, and see and act
    this noble knight.
Acted by age, acted by youth, acted on this stage
    tonight.
If you don't believe in what I say, walk in King George,
    and clear the way".

BACON CURING AT FARINGDON

The greatest part of the pigs slaughtered in Berkshire are made into bacon. About four thousand are killed at Faringdon alone between Michaelmas and April. They are cured in the usual way and dried, in proper store rooms, with wood or coal.

(*General Survey of the Agriculture of Berkshire*
by William Mavor)

15

The Berkshire Pig

Throughout the second half of the nineteenth century dairy farming remained the strongest section of agriculture in the Berkshire Vale and owing to the heavy falls in wheat prices in the second and third quarters of the century there was a growing abandonment of grain in favour of milk production.

The late 1870's saw the full effect of Sir Robert Peel's Repeal of the Corn Laws: a change from protectionism to the laissez-faire free-trade policy. Wet seasons — especially 1879 — coincided with increasing wheat production in Canada, South America, the United States of America and Russia. Much cheaper transport facilities permitted massive imports of inexpensive hard wheat to Britain causing a general depression — the so-called Great Agricultural Depression. The Wantage area was particularly affected. Tenants on the Lockinge Estate of Lord Wantage and Mr. Wroughton's Woolley Estate left the land and elsewhere farmers laid down permanent pasture and milk production increased rapidly.[1]

The Great Western Railway became an important artery for moving milk to Reading and Bristol, but especially to London. By the 1890's it was known as *The Milky Way* and twice a day churns of milk were crowded on station platforms between Didcot and Shrivenham. A natural complement to an increase in dairy farming was the rising importance of pig rearing and fattening on the waste, skimmed milk, the cream having been used for butter or cheese.

1 Estate Villages.

But to return to the earlier part of the nineteenth century: even then pig rearing was important in the Vale economy. Loveden's dairy farm at Buscot had attached to it a well-designed piggery. From the dairy skimmed-milk flowed directly into the pigs' troughs. Berkshire's special breed of pig which Loveden kept became world famous and commanded high prices at home and abroad as breeding stock. Black, compact, good feeders, they could hardly be bettered by any other breed and large numbers were sent to America and South Africa for breeding purposes.

An attempt to improve the breed took place about 1860 by crossing Berkshires with Suffolk and Sussex pigs. The projectors called them the Improved Berkshires but their experiment failed as the new breed was difficult to meat. The traditional type reasserted its supremacy. In 1885 the *British Berkshire Society* published pedigrees of the breed, while soon after an *American Berkshire Society* was founded and produced several additional pedigree books. The British volume records that from early times careful details of pedigrees were noted by breeders through numerous generations, and in all it holds five hundred and forty separate pedigrees. Among notable breeders were the society's secretary Mr. Humphrey of Shippon, Mr. John Walter, of Bear Wood, Lord Middleton and Mr. A. Hammond.

Loveden fed his Berkshire pigs not just on skimmed milk but with boiled potatoes, barley, beans and pulses. Other farmers fed the newly introduced Swedish turnip and a few used grain which had fermented for about six months. At Letcombe Bassett Mr. Smith studied pig breeding and decided it necessary to cross Berkshire animals once in six or seven years with Indian pigs to prevent them degenerating; for similar reasons Loveden crossed his animals with a Chinese or Tonquin race.

While the normal weight of animals was between ten and eighteen score, two notable pigs were bred in Berkshire: Loveden's hog was certainly only twenty-eight score but had a most extraordinary shape, while Mr. Butler's Hog of Tidmarsh Farm near Pangbourne, killed in 1797, weighed over forty score, was eight feet long and measured three feet seven and a half inches in height and had a nine foot girth.[2]

Pigs were processed — smoke dried — on most Vale farms. Farmhouses used wood smoke and here and there a special arrangement was made to cater for a larger number of sides. The Old Rectory at West Hanney, for instance, had a chamber built into the chimney above the fire to allow several sides to be smoked together, while at Farnborough Old Rectory a similar arrangement was in use. Even Loveden had a bacon house in which he always used coal smoke. At Faringdon about eight thousand sides were smoked annually prior to despatch to Oxford and London markets. The trade was shared by two families and their bacon had a deservedly high reputation. Because of the uncertainty of Thames navigation it was transported by road waggon. Wantage bacon was considered of superior quality to Faringdon's but by no means equal in quantity, while the many pigs bred and fattened in the neighbourhood of Wallingford were processed in the bacon houses there and sold partly through the local pork butchery businesses.

2   Mavor p.305.

AVERAGE PRICES OF CORN,
FROM THE RETURNS ENDING JAN. 22, 1803

	Wheat		Barley		Oats		Beans	
	s	d	s	d	s	d	s	d
Berkshire	58	6	23	11	21	10	33	7
Oxfordshire	54	1	21	11	19	1	32	10
Average for England & Wales per quarter	56	8	25	4	19	4	33	7

PRICES OF FLOUR, JANUARY 24, 1803

Fine	45s to 50s	Common Pollard	17s to 18s
Seconds	40s to 45s	Horse Pollard	24s
Middling	—	Bran	13s 6d
Fine Pollard	22s to 24s		

(*The Gentleman's Magazine*, January, 1803)

92

16

Mills and milling

Although the foundation of milling in England was laid in medieval times, the hey-day of the watermill was probably reached in the mid-Victorian years, following that era of rural development called the agricultural revolution. Berkshire is so well endowed with watercourses that from earliest times it boasted a considerable number of mills, and the north Berkshire rivers Ock, Thames and Lambourn, with the Ginge and Letcombe waterways, supported a procession of village mills. Most remain, although few are in use today, and some are in a sad state of repair. Nine mills on the Ginge brook still exist, the Letcombe brook and River Ock with its countless tributaries boasted eleven mills each, while the river Lambourn maintained a further ten watermills.

The miller had an important place in late-Victorian village life. In a substantially wheat and barley growing area, as the Vale was in the 1880's, the miller formed the essential link between the farmer and the baker, who provided one of the necessities of life to village families. His function was as important as the brewer's, carrier's or boot-maker's at a time when local self-sufficiency was still evident. The wholesale import of cheaper grain from north America which set off the great agricultural depression of the mid-1870's caused some change in the local wheat and barley growing emphasis, and a consequent movement into pastoral and beef farming. Nevertheless, the local millers survived, and it was often not until after 1914 that their businesses began to contract.

It is fair to generalise that most north Berkshire mills had undershot wheels and worked a pair of millstones. Usually made of sandstone or grit and of varying dimensions, they were often between three and four feet in diameter and about six inches thick, with a pattern incised on their flat surface to a depth of about an inch. Along the Letcombe brook at Wantage three mills flourished. Upstream was the Ham mill, in 1860 kept by Thomas Stevens then Willoughby's mill kept by James Willoughby, and the largest was Clark's Town Mill at the foot of Mill Street, having advantages of closeness to the Wantage arm of the Wilts & Berks canal. Grain and flour were moved on the canal arm between 1810 and its closure in 1906. During the Wantage tramway's active lifespan of 1875 to about 1943 it increasingly took over from the canal as the mill's main outlet and access route.

Upstream from Wantage were the three Letcombe mills and downstream two Grove mills. In the 1860's Grove upper mill was worked by Mrs Mary Anne Hine and Lower mill by Henry Lay. Upper, or Cane Lane mill, is neatly refurbished as a dwelling house but has losts its milling gear, but Lower mill was demolished a few years ago to make way for housing development. A little further downstream East Hanney's two mills ceased active work in the early 1920's. West's mill is a relatively modern structure on an old mill site, and from the top floor there are splendid views to be had over the orchards which surround the Hanneys. Some of the mill workings remain — there are trap doors through which sacks of grain were hauled up four floors; there is the gantry from which pulleys and ropes unloaded waggons waiting below, and to one side is the cut-off stream to take flood water; but the most important portion, the wheel, has been removed. About 1865 the miller here was Henry Hall.

It was common for local watermills to be used at some time in their lives for other purposes, and this was true of West's mill where a silk weaving business was carried on during the Napoleonic wars, manned by French prisoners from the great silk manufacturing town of Lyons, but the short-lived activity quickly died out when they returned to France and the mill resumed its traditional uses.

In this late-Victorian period and in the opening years of the twentieth century, the two villages and surrounding countryside found sufficient work for both Hanney mills to flourish, but at one stage East Hanney's second mill, Dandridge's mill, which in the 1860's was worked by Patrick Thomas, also experienced a temporary change of use and was devoted to woollen cloth manufacture.

The greatest quantity of milling gear remaining in north Berkshire probably survives in Venn mill which is downstream from East Hanney and is the last mill on the Letcombe brook. The undershot wheel is almost twelve feet in diameter and is well preserved having metal paddles and spokes. The timber gearing is still connected to a set of grinding stones on first floor level. This mill was active until after the Second World War which accounts for the degree of preservation of the mechanism.

Of other mills in the area, Sutton Courtenay's Upper mill on the Ginge brook was easily the largest in the village, having a couple of pairs of grinding stones, but the New Cut mill at Sutton Wick on the river Ock has been turned into a dwelling, while Drayton mill had four pairs of millstones and a fine wheel with dished spokes and for many years, along with Milton mill, was kept by the Bradfield family.

Charney Bassett had a small mill on the river Ock with an undershot wheel some ten feet in diameter. Some grinding gears remain along with an uncommon covered area on the roadside for unloading waggons. On the southern side an overflow channel and weir with paddles is still largely intact. Many mills are now private houses; a century ago they were also bustling centres of an essential agricultural activity, such places as Dry Sandford mill, Marcham mill, Stanford-in-the-Vale mill on the main Wantage to Faringdon turnpike, Charney Bassett mill, Venn mill on the Besselsleigh turnpike between East Hanney and Garford, Steventon mill, Prior's mill at Blewbury and two of Hendred's three mills — the third, Ludbridge mill, was demolished in 1963.

Dry Sandford mill situated on the slight stream of the Sandford brook at Cothill was probably one of the more unusual working mills in the area in the late nineteenth century for it had a large overshot wheel some ten feet in diameter. Several mill stones lie scattered around the garden, all of average size, but some have strong metal bindings round their edges. This mill, like so many others in the Vale, ceased active life in the early 1920's, and around one door initials and dates indicate former millers. The earliest was carved in 1617, while a partnership of E.T. and I.G. apparently worked the mill in 1734. Other inscriptions and dates include P.N. 1872 and R.W. 1879.

As one might expect, Abingdon was well supplied with milling capacity, and St. Helen's mill, the Ock mill and Bug's mill on the edge of Abingdon Common were all thriving concerns in the later part of the nineteenth century. St. Helen's mill was particularly well sited being close to the Wilts and Berks canal entry to the river Thames wharf and had a considerable river trade up to London. The oldest Abingdon mill — and one of England's oldest — was the Abbey mill. As its name indicates, it was more than a mere manorial mill, and was a very flourishing commercial enterprise in the fifteenth century when Abingdon Abbey's harvest from the vast local estates was ground here. As a milling enterprise it worked well into the nineteenth century, and in its heyday boasted two waterwheels and seven pairs of grinding stones.

THE OLD BERKSHIRE HOUNDS
A PEEP AT THE BERKSHIRE

Just chancing this morning through Brightwell to stray,
I suddenly heard 'Tally-ho!' 'Gone away!'
When quick in a body the 'Berkshire' flew by,
Their fox just away, and 'Forward' 's the cry;
Two hundred horsemen in the scene take a part,
All cramming or nicking to get a good start,
See! who have we here on that fiery steed,
Who o'er hedge and brook seems determined to lead?
'Tis 'Dare-devil George' who thus heads the throng;
'Old Billy', as usual, well lurking along.
That style not a moment while running he'll slack,
Then go across country the nearest way back;
And this happy task, proh pudor! I speak,
Master Billy performs about three days a week.

With elbows well squared and without any noise,
But quiet and cool comes the Lord of Camoys;
Who just for a day has deserted Sir John,
To see how the Berkshire affairs are going on.

Behind him, his voice rising higher and higher,
And all in a bustle, comes Brightwell's great squire.
'By G-d, sir, what hounds! they can do the trick;
I wish those cursed Tories like this we could lick:
Master Morland must put us now in the front rank,
For Brightwell ne'er yet knew the meaning of blank.

'Dare-devil George' was Mr George Montague, who was
afterwards Master of the South Berks. 'Good-natured Billy'
was a son of Mr Lowndes, 'Brightwell's great Squire,' who
was an ardent Whig. 'Sir John' was Sir John Cope, then
hunting the countries now known as South Berks and Mr
Garth's.

(*Old Berkshire Hunt* by L. C. Loder-Symonds)

BERKSHIRE BREED.

33

34

Mr Chas Butler's Berkshire Hog

STEVENTON CAUSEWAY.

35

36

STEVENTON MILL.

39

4

41

42

43

44

45

46

BOAT-HOUSE, ABINGDON.

47

48

49

50

51

52

53

54

55

56

57

58

59

60

61

62

64

3

65

66

67

17

Fox hunting

As a pursuit for country gentlemen, fox-hunting developed throughout the eighteenth and nineteenth centuries on exclusive, expensive and parochial lines. Its place in the annual sporting round was very minor — even in the nineteenth century cock fighting, prize fighting and duelling frequently attracted greater public attention than did the farmers, squires and nobles enjoying the chase.

In north Berkshire the Vale country was hunted for fox continuously from 1760; consequently the Old Berkshire Hunt is one of England's oldest, even though it hunted under its present name only from 1809.

Among the early masters of a recognisable local pack is the Rev. Thomas Loder, Rector and Lord of the Manor at Hinton Waldrist. His country was largely confined to the Longworth and Faringdon area but occasionally meets took place north of the Thames at Cokethorpe Covert.

Back in 1766 the Earl of Abingdon wrote a verse account of a record-breaking run lasting for over five hours. Loder's hounds ran from Longworth out to Beedon, on to Donnington and back to Catmore where it was reported the fox escaped by jumping into a church. The seal of approval was set upon Loder's pack by the Earl when in 1784 his pack, which had been kept for generations by the family, was amalgamated with Loder's. Consolidation by Loder was continued by the Rev. Robert Symonds who took the mastership in 1800 and hunted much the same country. Nevertheless disagreements frequently occurred between the masters of adjacent hunts and soon Symonds and his supporters were accused of poaching territory; the result of this first encounter was the division of the country by the Wantage to Faringdon road.

A whole series of short masterships followed; William Codrington took over, then Harvey Combe, followed by Lord Kintore of Wadley House, Littleworth. Kintore hunted the Vale much more widely than his predecessors had done. *The Sporting Magazine* in 1827 commented that his favourite country was normally in the area of Kingston Lisle, Uffington, Little Coxwell and Stanford-in-the-Vale. Yet another bitter disagreement arose with the Hon. Henry Morton's mastership because Sir John Cope and Mr. T. T. Morland, of Abingdon, hunted regularly from Marcham Park and covered the whole eastern portion of the Vale country. A meeting at Faringdon's Crown Inn in 1832 was convened to solve the difficulty, and a plan evolved for the area bounded by Burford, Oxford, Highclere and Marlborough to be hunted exclusively by the original pack. To Morland and Cope this was clearly intolerable and resulted in the division of the Vale of the White Horse into the Old Berkshire country based on Marcham and the Vale of the White Horse Hunt based on Cricklade. Consequently Morland and his friends continued to hunt the lower Ock Vale and this precedent was continued by Lord Radnor, who in 1833 became master.

The area of the Old Berks was extended by Thomas Thornhill Morland (master 1835-47) in return for subscriptions amounting to £1,000 a year. From Faringdon the region stretched to Henley, the kennels were moved to Sandford, and the Oxfordshire country around Shotover was added to the Old Berks.

Another disagreement, marked as always by a volume of correspondence between the parties, occurred in 1835 and resulted in the South Oxfordshire Hunt under the leadership of the Earl of Macclesfield being formed. At this time Morland was keeping at bay adjacent hunts on two sides; not only Macclesfield's party but also the Cricklade hunt. These factors, coupled with severe injuries suffered in a carriage accident and continued illness, forced him to retire in 1847. The man who took over was James Morrell, whose father founded the Oxford Brewery. For over ten years he hunted the Abingdon to Ilsley area, but when he

100

succeeded to the family business he moved to Tubney House and kept the hounds there in the spacious kennels. Shortly after the move *The Field* records that Mr. Tattersall auctioned the pack, twenty-five hounds fetching 484 guineas and the whole sale realising 6,127 guineas.

The mastership, once again open, was taken by C. P. Duffield, of Marcham Park, who was related to the celebrated miser John Elwes who had hunted from Marcham some time earlier.[1] Also like Elwes, Duffield became a Member of Parliament for Abingdon but resigned to make way for Sir Frederick Thesiger, the Solicitor-General who failed to get elected elsewhere.

Possibly resulting from the high cost of hunting, a couple of joint-masterships took the country: first Thomas Duffield and the Earl of Craven; then C. P. Duffield with V. W. Van de Weyer hunted the country after £2,000 had been subscribed. At this time a committee was formed to build new kennels at Kingston Bagpuize. Eventually John Wheeler of Wantage built them to designs by F. H. Barfield of Faringdon. The hunt headquarters remained there until well into the present century.

This joint-mastership was very popular Van de Weyer was a Belgian diplomat, being Minister-Plenipotentiary to St. James' Palace. In north Berkshire he met widely and often. One of the best hunts on record through the cream of the Old Berkshire country resulted from a meet at the Blowingstone in March 1886. The hounds ran from Kingston Lisle to Uffington Wood, then to Woolstone, over the canal near Childrey, along the railway beyond Goosey and Denchworth, and across Grove level-crossing to Woodhill where hounds and horses gave up the chase exhausted.

Slightly over ten years after Van de Weyer's retirement some of the first Hunt Point-to-Point races took place. In 1902 a joint meeting with Cricklade Hunt was held at Highworth where both Subscribers' Cup and Farmers' Cup were won by Old Berks members. The Old Berks held its own races in 1904 at Barcote Manor between Buckland and

1 *Eight Men of Berkshire* pp.6-8.

101

Littleworth. Between two and three thousand spectators saw the races, and beforehand a luncheon was given for over five hundred farmers from the neighbourhood. The Point-to-Points remain important events in the Hunt Calendars and the Old Berks meeting now takes place on the Berkshire Downs above Lockinge.

TOLLS ON THE OXFORD TO ABINGDON TURNPIKE

The scale of tolls for Hinksey and Folly Bridge between Oxford and Abingdon is given:- For every coach, chariot, landau, berlin, chaise, calash, chair, hearse, litter, or other carriage whatsoever (except waggons, wains or carts) with four wheels,

	s.	d.
Drawn by six horses	*2*	*0*
Drawn by four horses	*1*	*8*
Drawn by three horses	*1*	*6*
Drawn by two horses	*1*	*0 &c.*

(*Jackson's Oxford Journal*, January 9th 1819)

18

Lanes, turnpikes, bridges and ferries

I have walked out of Wantage to West Hanney along a track that has not seen regular transport for close on two hundred years. The whole of north Berkshire is still criss-crossed by a spider's web of old roads which were once vital lines of communication between neighbouring villages and the local towns. In the hills shepherds drove their sheep along them while in the Vale herdsmen moved cattle and pigs to market and villagers followed on foot and horseback. Turnpikes usually caused these green lanes to be abandoned by through traffic, but even in the late-nineteenth century they continued in use by isolated farmsteads and villages.

The old road along which I passed was a main route from Wantage to Oxford before the turnpike was built by the Besselsleigh Turnpike Trust in 1770. Down Mill Street the road turns off to link with today's Denchworth road, and unmade stretches of green lane can be seen across Grove airfield marked by parallel rows of trees. To the west of Grove village Cane lane, Brook lane and Townsend join the route, and almost opposite Brook lane a junction led off to Denchworth. On from Grove Wick Green the track varies in width. Here thirty feet broad, a few hundred yards on it has narrowed to fifteen feet or less, and is everywhere bordered by rows of solid elms. Opposite Monk's Farm and shortly before the railway, the track again divides. One lane emerges on the public road opposite Aldworth's in West Hanney, after being joined by a second route from

Denchworth. The other lane passes on by Grove Wick Farm and Bradfield Grove to pass between East and West Hanney.

If you ever try to follow this route take a look at Bradfield Grove for the solid old cottages, built well before the present farmhouse, which face west towards the early route and stand about a hundred yards back from the lane. Today the only access is from the opposite side so that the drive passes through a yard before it reaches the former farmhouse — consequently the whole settlement pattern is reversed.

The remainder of the Oxford road passes south of Garford, by the Noah's Ark (beside which is yet another old route) to Frilford, Oakley and Cothill, then into the city either by way of Wootton, Hen Wood, North Hinksey and Osney, or over Foxcombe Hill and down past Chiswell Farm and South Hinksey. This section of the road from Frilford to Oxford was turnpiked mainly in 1768. Further turnpikes in the region include the Faringdon, Wantage, Wallingford road (1752) and the Faringdon, Abingdon, Shillingford turnpike to Henley and London (1733). Naturally this connected westwards from Faringdon with the Lechlade and Fairford road (1726), and on to Cirencester then Gloucester.[1]

The Tithe map of West Hanney (1844)[2] gives a helpful indication of the road pattern in the village. Today's Denchworth road halted at the Childrey brook. To get to Denchworth one took a mud track south-west from the village by Aldworths. Grass Roads extended round the south of the village to rickyards behind the church ending in Butt's Piece. One interesting point is the extensive village green which then stretched northwards towards the back of Rectory Farm and parallel to Winter Lane. At the northern end two ponds pointed along the green to the south. They have now been filled in but in the undergrowth can still be traced in outline.

1 The Oxford Region p.126.
2 In Bodleian Library Oxford.

Old roads abound in other regions. To reach Long Wittenham from Appleford one now makes a three-mile detour southwards away from the river, but a couple of centuries ago the route was more direct: wheeled vehicles and foot travellers passed up by Appleford church and entered Wittenham at the western end — distance one mile.

Similarly there is an approximate rectangle of roads cornered by Abingdon, Frilford, Wantage and Rowstock with only the Steventon to Hanney road crossing it. Around 1750 the situation was much different. One could travel from Abingdon directly to Wantage along a road which roughly took the line of the old Wilts and Berks Canal. From Sutton Wick was a route to Bug's Mill on the Ock; one joined the Wantage road at Frog Moor Elm, while from Drayton another passed north-westwards to Marcham Mill — then called Werg Mill — and Marcham village. Out from Drayton passed other routes. One crossed to East Hanney by Landmead Farm while another divided Steventon Mead and Common to join the Hanney road near the canal bridge. In the area of Grove Park the road pattern when judged by today's standards was quite unrecognisable; a devious route leading eventually to Oxford passed down the main street. From Grove bridge another road wound over Crab Hill to Charlton while others crossed King's Grove Common to Knowls's Farm, Tulwick, Windsor and Pinmarsh on the old Abingdon route. From West Lockinge and Ardington parallel lanes dropped to the Vale and eventually joined this same Abingdon road, while from West Hendred a track cut down beside the Ginge brook into Steventon, forming part of an early pack-horse track from Hungerford through Shefford, Woolley, Farnborough, Hendred and Steventon leading to Abingdon. The Pack Horse inn above Steventon Hill was associated with a further route from the hills through East Hendred and Milton to Abingdon, which in addition may have served as a drove road, along which cattle and sheep were herded to market. The Ridgeway and Icknield Way, together with countless other downland green roads, certainly served this purpose; for instance, those tracks radiating from East Ilsley had an important function as cattle and sheep roads at local market and fair times.[3]

North of Abingdon several roads led to Radley through Northcott, Barton and Thorpe, linking Wick and Pumney farms with the town. Radley itself was somewhat isolated by the meander of the Thames, the closest river crossing being a ferry near Nuneham lock. Another road took a route from Warren house above Culham over the Thames cut to Andersey island, and by way of Rye farm entered Abingdon at Burford bridge. Further Thames crossing points were scarce, and clearly controlled routes out of north Berkshire. The old bridges, of considerable strategic importance during the civil war, remained at Radcot, Lechlade, Kingston Bagpuize, Oxford, Abingdon, Culham and Wallingford. Elsewhere ferries supplemented the bridges at Bablock Hythe, Long Wittenham and Shillingford, but as turnpikes developed extra bridges were built. Swinford bridge replaced a ferry in 1767 to carry the Oxford, Eynsham and Burford Turnpike (1751) over the river: 1802 saw Tadpole bridge link Bampton with Buckland and by 1767 a wooden bridge appeared at Shillingford to be replaced in 1827 by an ornamental stone bridge.[4] The six russet-coloured arches which span the Thames at Clifton Hampden replaced a ferry in 1864. This narrow but graceful bridge, with its former toll-house on the Berkshire bank, was designed by Sir Gilbert Scott and built from coarse bricks hand-made in the locality on Lord Aldenham's estate.

Country roads before the piecemeal improvement of the turnpike system were in a grim state: winter quagmires became bone-hard rutted tracks in high summer. Arthur Young, who was first secretary of the Board of Agriculture, wrote voluminous letters and journals describing his travels and called local pre-turnpike roads formidable, but by about 1809 it was said that a noble change had taken place in their condition. By accepting the principle that users should contribute to road upkeep, the parish was no longer

3 See Rocque *Map of Berkshire* 1761 for detail.
4 *The Oxford Region* p.127.

faced with the impossible task of repairing surfaces of busy main roads which happened to cross its boundaries. The turnpike trusts led to a marked improvement in administration, repair and structure, and this despite frequently violent opposition to payment of tolls.

Local turnpike trusts were established to improve the main roads as follows: Faringdon to Lechlade and Fairford, 1726; Faringdon to Wantage and Wallingford, 1752; Faringdon to Besselsleigh, 1733; Abingdon to Kingston Bagpuize, 1755; Oxford to Abingdon, Shillingford and Henley, 1733 and Wantage to Besselsleigh in 1770.

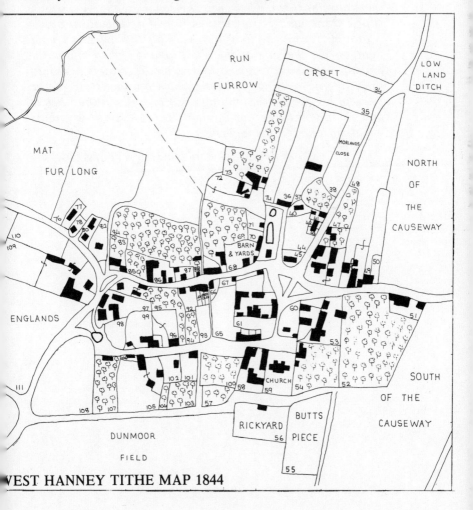

WEST HANNEY TITHE MAP 1844

THE WILTSHIRE AND BERKSHIRE CANAL
AT UFFINGTON

The White Horse Vale, remember, was traversed by no great road; nothing but country parish roads, and these very bad. Only one coach ran there, and this one only from Wantage to London so that the western part of the vale was without regular means of moving on, and certainly didn't seem to want them. There was the canal, by the way, which supplied the country-side with coal, and up and down which continually went the long barges, with the big black men lounging by the side of the horses along the towing-path, and the women in bright-coloured handkerchiefs standing in the sterns steering. Standing I say, but you could never see whether they were standing or sitting, all but their heads and shoulders being out of sight in the cosy little cabins which occupied some eight feet of the stern.

(*Tom Brown's School Days*, by Thomas Hughes)

19

The canal era

One of nineteenth-century north Berkshire's more memorable red-letter days occurred on a bright September afternoon in 1810, when the Wiltshire and Berkshire canal was finally opened for navigation. Abingdon's St Helen's wharf was a scene of gaiety and make-merry. It must have been a splendid sight as those decorated narrow barges, with music playing and banners flying, passed down the canal, through the final lock and into the Thames.

Likewise, the buildings and streets in the centre of Abingdon were bedecked with garlands and streamers, and the market place seethed with people. To one side a group of local gentry, distinguished landowners, Bristol and London businessmen, canal company officials, and Members of Parliament for half-a-dozen canal-side constituencies, many of whom had put up money to help finance the venture, entered the council chamber to partake of a gigantic celebration dinner. Towards the end of the proceedings the chairman duly proposed "Success to the Wiltshire and Berkshire Canal", and the company, highly gratified, separated at a late hour. The venture was off to a good start, although the final cost of construction was in excess of £250,000.

Disaster had at first threatened, and building the canal had proved a long struggle. First mooted in 1793 at a meeting in Swindon, it was seven years before the canal could carry barges to Chippenham, Calne then Wootton Bassett from Bath. Three years later a wharf was completed at Swindon, and by December 1805 navigation was possible to Longcot. But north Berkshire waited another five years for the canal to be dug across the Vale, running through Grove, East Hanney, Drayton, then finally to its end at

Abingdon, in length fifty-two miles incorporating forty-two locks. It had a depth of four feet six inches, had a bottom width of thirteen feet six inches and a water surface width of twenty-seven feet. Each barge, seventy feet long and seven feet broad, was intended to carry about twenty-five tons of cargo. Had the canal been a larger size suitable for transporting Thames barges, it would have been economically viable and a very productive concern.[1]

Many difficulties had been faced and overcome, and the opening was an historic event for the White Horse Vale because the Wilts and Berks canal was the area's sole contribution to the canal mania which raged in England between 1790 and 1815. Throughout the country canals cut were few compared with those projected, and in the Abingdon area there were numerous plans and schemes, each one accompanied by its public meeting for landowners and interested parties to voice their opinion and for money to be raised, but matters rarely went further. One such plan was for a canal to link Lechlade and Abingdon, passing near Faringdon, shortening the Thames barge route by cutting off that great swing in the river between Radcot and Abingdon. The year was 1784, but progress was unbelievably slow and the scheme was eventually dropped.

In spite of earlier failure, enthusiasm for canal cutting rose again the following year with a suggested waterway from Stratford-on-Avon to Witney and Newbridge, then by way of Fyfield and Marcham to meet the Thames at Abingdon. But this time opposition was violent and sustained. Landowners considered it "as highly injurious to the tract of country through which it proposes to pass". Even Abingdon's Member of Parliament was caught up in the storm of indignation which ensued. In the Borough Edward Loveden, MP was persistently attacked for acquiescing in the destructive canal schemes. The reason for Loveden's desire to build canals was almost certainly private profit. Below his Buscot home he built new wharves to take a string of Thames barges. For much of his life he was concerned with sending cheese and farm produce to

1   Mavor p.447.

110

London — an exceedingly lucrative business — and clearly any scheme such as a canal for shortening the river journey would add to Loveden's income; little wonder he was such a staunch champion of canals to Abingdon.

Another scheme, under discussion between 1810 and 1817, was for an extension from Abingdon to Aylesbury to link with the Grand Union canal. A possible line was surveyed in 1819 and a cast-iron viaduct proposed to take the canal over the Thames; the whole scheme for a Western Junction canal as it was to be called, fell into abeyance by 1828; it was to have shared in the lucrative coal trade of the Wilts & Berks canal. The Thames Commissioners in 1811 printed their own case against the canal schemes, particularly the proposed Wilts and Berks extensions from Sutton Courtenay to Aylesbury and Marshworth; from Swindon to Latton and from Abingdon through Newbridge and Witney to Stratford-on-Avon.

They said that the Thames from Abingdon to Lechlade would not be navigable in summer months "because the sources of the Isis will be diverted by the canal from Swindon to Latton and the bed of the river will thus become a morass, and pernicious to the health of the inhabitants of its banks". In winter months they felt the river would not be navigable "from Lechlade to Abingdon because it is intended to build an aqueduct from Sutton to Culham for the use of the canal from Abingdon to Aylesbury, which will obstruct the floods from going off — the lowlands will thus be considerably damaged, and the river Thame will be carried in a new channel from Buckinghamshire across the county of Oxford into Berkshire."

A reply in favour of the schemes came from *A real friend of the City of Oxford and to Truth* on January 23rd 1811, addressed to the University and inhabitants of the City of Oxford, on the line of the intended Western Junction Canal. It would enable cheap Somerset coal to reach Thame, would reduce coal prices in Oxford and would act as a useful check on the Oxford Canal Company. Another reply, from *A friend of the Old River*, was dated January 29th 1811. "Was not the Wilts & Berks Canal made under the

111

express promise that the goods brought along the canal should be carried down the River Thames to London? To effectuate such a carriage down the river were not many of the improvements below Abingdon, where the Wilts & Berks Canal enters the Thames, and in particular, the Cut at Culham, which cost upwards of £5,000, undertaken and made at the special desire of the persons interested in the canal? Trade, he said would be diverted from the Thames into canals leading to the annihilation of the trade on the river." [2]

But in numerous ways the Wilts and Berks canal was of benefit to north Berkshire and an arm similar to the Calne, Chippenham and Longcot branches was dug to link Wantage to the main channel. Prosperity in the canalside towns soared; by 1850 Wantage had a cloth-mill, four rope works, four tanneries, several chandleries and an iron factory. Abingdon had a similar range of industries but could add several grain mills to the list, while at East Challow the iron foundry was sited right on the canal bank to give cheap transport for its bulky merchandise. Abingdon became the busiest coal wharf at the eastern half of the canal. By the late 1830's over 10,000 tons of coal a year were unloaded there, with about 2,000 tons a year at both Challow and Wantage. A further 3,300 tons were unloaded at Longcot wharf for transport to Faringdon. [3]

Despite the rise in prosperity, one great disadvantage came with the canal: it allowed hordes of navvies who had dug the waterways to remain in the area, and many more shady and unsavoury characters filtered from London and the northern cities into the canalside towns. Wantage became so notorious that it was soon called *Black Wantage* — a haunt of sundry criminals. Bear-baiting, dog-fighting, cock-fighting, and bull-baiting often took place in the unpaved, ill-lit, and narrow alleyways which led off from the market place in a maze of crooked lanes. Fighting and drunkenness in the abundant inns were everyday sights. But matters went from bad to worse, and by 1828 had reached

2 Documents in Bodleian Library Oxford.
3 Hadfield p.287.

112

such a pitch that a special Act of Parliament *for Lighting, Watching, Cleansing, Paving and otherwise improving the Town of Wantage in the County of Berks* was passed. Running to one hundred and four clauses, it laid down conditions in greatest detail providing for every eventuality. The nightwatchmen who called "past twelve o'clock and a cloudy night" or "past five o'clock and a fine morning" were replaced by two silent keepers of the dark hours, while further clauses ordered how "Nuisances, Annoyances, and Obstructions" were to be handled. A fire engine was kept in the church porch under control of the vestry committee, and as a fire prevention measure thatching new houses and renewing thatch on others was forbidden. People's freedom was severely curtailed: for instance, nobody in the town was allowed to "run, draw, haul, drive, drag, or carry any Truck, Wheel, Sledge, Wheelbarrow, Bier, Handbarrow, or any other carriage". Owners and occupiers of town houses were ordered to keep their hedges neatly trimmed. Theirs also was the responsibility for cleanliness of the streets and alleys. The Act did appoint a scavenger but washing and other waste liquids could not be allowed to run into any "River, Brook, or Running Stream, Well, Ditch, Pond, Canal, Sewer, or Conduit", and furthermore individuals were ordered to sweep regularly the footpaths outside their houses and in winter to clear all ice and snow.

And what of the men who worked the canal in its hey-day? Although few records remain, one colourful personality is still remembered. He was the lock-keeper at Grove; Mr Jimmy Bradshaw stood well over six feet tall and could often be seen beside the canal wearing his black peaked cap, sailor fashion, a bright red spotted scarf round his neck, and a lengthy tail coat below it. His home backed on to the canal just above Grove Bridge, and a wharf-side terrace nearby still bears the name Canal Cottages, although the waterway has long since gone.

As one might suspect, Thomas Hughes gives a picture of the old canal. It was then the only regular transport in the western part of the Vale, and supplied the countryside with coal from those "long barges, with the big black men lounging by the side of the horses along the towing-path, and the women in bright-coloured handkerchiefs standing in the sterns steering." Nanny had told Tom Brown that these women were in the habit of "enticing children into the barges and taking them up to London and selling them," which Tom naturally refused to believe.

Abingdon too became more prosperous, for it evolved as a waterways centre with branches to Bristol, Birmingham, and London. Each week fully-laden barges set out from Temple Backs in Bristol and from London. Twice a week gaily-painted regular-passage craft carrying coal, timber, grain, and pottery plied between Abingdon and the Wilts and berks wharf at Bath. The canal also moved finished bricks and tiles from the Childrey and Challow kilns sited near the canal side, while semi-finished materials and manufactured goods were likewise moved from the Challow foundry. In the 1830's a flyboat service carried passengers quickly between Abingdon, Bath and Bristol. There was a further express passenger service from London through Abingdon to Gloucester and from Oxford through Banbury to Birmingham.

In many ways the Wilts & Berks Canal was a master routeway which near Swindon linked Abingdon to the Thames and Severn canal between Sharpness and Lechlade by the North Wilts canal. At Semington the Wilts and Berks canal joined the Kennet and Avon canal and at Bradford-on-Avon a junction arm linked Timsbury and Radstock on the Somerset Coal canal to the main system. Hence coal from Somerset could quite easily be transported up the Vale for sale in Abingdon. Further indication of the wide area to the north which could be reached by canal from Abingdon appeared in an advertisement of 1814 in *Jackson's Oxford Journal*. It announced "Goods intended for Oxford, Witney, Banbury, Burford, Warwick, Coventry, Birmingham, and other parts of the north of England are regularly forwarded from Abingdon; and goods from these places and the Potteries will be carried to Bath and Bristol, or any of the above-named places." What a pity it was dug as a narrow-boat canal!

Today we are reconciled to high fares, and by present standards freight rates on the canal in 1815 seem incredibly low. From Abingdon a manufacturer could send a ton of goods to London or Bristol for a mere £1.5s (£1.25). It could go to Wantage for five shillings (25p); to Swindon for seven shillings (35p); and to Bath for only 16s 8d (83p).

Cheaper coal reached Abingdon and Wantage from South Wales, and from Timsbury and Radstock on the Somerset coalfield, fetched on the Wilts and Berks canal; it could undercut the price charged for Tyne coal brought up river from London, and for Staffordshire and West Midland coal brought to the area by the Oxford canal. In return the canal shipped grain from Abingdon and the Vale towns to Bath and Bristol. In 1837 over 43,000 tons of Somerset coal were moved on the canal and that year more than five thousand barge journeys were made in both directions.[4] All round, the canals had the effect of speeding transport, cutting costs, and bringing many isolated districts into civilisation, but the days of waterways were numbered.

It is not too difficult to realise why the great canal era died when the railways came. Faster and cheaper transport for both goods and passengers came to the Vale of the White Horse in 1840 with the Great Western Railway line between London and Bristol. The towns, once reliant upon the canal, were soon linked to the railway; Abingdon was joined in 1856, Faringdon in 1864, and Wantage by her tramway in 1875. And so the old canal, after serving the district well for over fifty years, went into honoured retirement in 1906 and was abandoned in 1914; today it remains as little more than a slight furrow in the flat landscape of the Vale, and as a short period in the history of north Berkshire.

4 Hadfield Canals of South and South-east England pp.276-294.

   Hadfield, Introducing Canals p.211.

DELAYS BEYOND DIDCOT

Beyond Didcot, great exertions have been made to complete the line for opening to a point near Faringdon simultaneously with the opening to Reading, and there can be no doubt that this might have been accomplished during May, possibly even April, had the season permitted it. A few weeks will complete the earth-work . . . and ballasting. If no further delays should now occur from the indirect consequences of the late wet season, the opening to Faringdon may be calculated upon in June or the beginning of July.

(I. K. Brunel's *Report*, February, 1840)

20

Travel and transport by railway

It was 1833, and landowners in southern England, from London to Bristol, were apprehensive and angry. The reason was that the Great Western Company had just published plans for a new trunk rail route. Property owners in the Home Counties met the Provost and Fellows of Eton to discuss action to overcome the railway threat. Townspeople in Windsor, Maidenhead, and Slough were shocked by the proposal, opinion in Oxford was faintly surprised, while the reaction of that innately conservative institution, the University, was completely predictable.

The prospectus clause which these parties disliked was the actual line of the railway "which will pass through or near Slough, Reading, Wantage, Swindon . . . a branch only twelve miles over a level country may connect the main line with Oxford." Eventually Bills passed both Houses of Parliament; some landlords had been bought off by sufficiently high compensation, and construction began. By March 1840, the first trains were running between Paddington and Reading, but the Berkshire town was not for long the western terminus of the Great Western Railway, and the line east of Pangbourne was inaugurated soon after.

Up the Vale west of Didcot and as far as Uffington relatively light work was completed quickly. Sir Isambard Brunel's report on this part of the line tells us some problems the railroad makers encountered. "Beyond Reading up to Didcot, a distance of 17½ miles, the ballasting is completely finished with the exception of two short lengths . . . the difficulty of procuring ballast for this

117

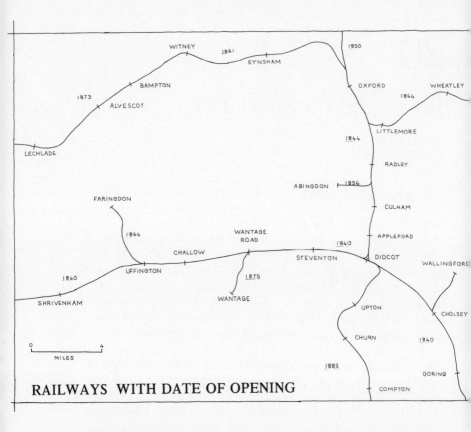

RAILWAYS WITH DATE OF OPENING

part of the line has been very great; the ground purchased for this purpose being underwater, it has been necessary to resort to dredging the river to obtain good gravel."[1] The cuttings, long waterfilled gullies beside the main line between Grove and Steventon, are a consequence of digging for ballast to put the railway on a fifteen-foot-high embankment across Grove Park. West of Didcot the permanent way was progressing, "a single line being laid for fifteen miles upon which the materials for the second line are carried to all parts, so that the work can proceed rapidly." West of Grove the Wilts and Berks canal was used to carry materials for construction of the railway line; the railway then quickly took over the canal's function as a carrier.

1 MacDermot p.53.

118

The line from Reading to Steventon was opened on June 1st 1840, and at the same time Pangbourne, Goring and Wallingford Road Stations were opened, but when the Wallingford branch was first used in 1866 the old station was renamed Moulsford and by 1892 superseded by a new station named Cholsey and Moulsford. In 1840 Steventon was in effect the station for Oxford, only ten miles away by the turnpike road, and to 1844 it kept this position by means of a frequent waggon and coach service. Even as recently as 1927 Steventon was used by Oxford for a large part of the night mails, and it could have become an important junction, initially for the Abingdon and Oxford line, had not landowners objected to the railway crossing their land. As it was, the Oxford branch ultimately missed Abingdon altogether and joined the trunk route at Didcot, a station actually opened four years after Steventon had been thriving from the Oxford trade. Early planners had sought to turn Oxford into the railway junction and to give it the major series of workshops which Swindon now possesses.

By July 20th 1840, the line extended to Faringdon Road, renamed Challow in 1864 by the opening of the Faringdon branch line to Uffington. Wantage Road Station was working in 1846 but was connected to Wantage by the steam tramway only 1875. Faringdon Road Station itself was in an important position on the main Gloucester, Cirencester and Cheltenham road, and the opening of the railway to some extent reduced road traffic towards London, but so far as Bristol and Bath were concerned goods and passengers still used the old London road through Marlborough and took the train from Reading, but opening the line to Temple Meads, Bristol, soon altered all this.

It was at Faringdon Road that one of the first recorded railway accidents on this line took place, and by chance Isambard Brunel was there to witness it. As he paced the windswept platform in the darkness early in the morning of Sunday, October 25th 1840, waiting for an engine to take him to London, he saw a light goods train approaching at an unusually high speed. In spite of his shouts and the efforts of the guard who was in the open truck behind the engine with four third-class passengers, the train rushed on and through the closed doors of the temporary engine shed, demolishing the building. The driver of the *Fire King* was killed, and four others, including the guard were injured. It appears that the driver was at the time asleep; one can only imagine how long the unfortunate man had been on duty.

A glance at a timetable and fare list at this period is quite enlightening. Between Paddington and Steventon in 1841 there was roughly a two-hourly service. The first train left the metropolis at 6 am and the last at 8.57 pm. The journey took less than two hours — the 6 am train being due to reach Steventon at 7.55 am.

Fares from Wallingford Road to London were unbelievably low: first class was only 11s 6d (57½p); second class 8s (40p); and third class 4s 6d (22½p), and for the benefit of passengers from a distance who joined the railway after a road journey, the company would willingly transport coaches and horses. A four-wheeled coach from Faringdon Road up to London cost 36s (£1.80p), a two-wheeler 27s (£1.35p), and the horses could be moved for 32s (£1.60p).

The Oxford branch shown in the original prospectus of 1833 caused a good deal of trouble, but no action came until 1836. A report in that year stated that "a branch line to Oxford and continuation to Worcester are promoted by the leading interests of those cities."[2] But still no action was taken; 1837 came and went: eventually a Bill was promoted in Parliament for a branch to Oxford. From Didcot it was to run to Cowley Road with a terminus near Magdalen Bridge, and a short branch to Abingdon, but this scheme was very strenuously opposed by Christ Church who owned part of the land.

Brunel altered the station site to Folly Bridge with an alternative in St. Clement's. The Bill passed the House of Commons but was defeated in the Lords with the aid of Peers acting for Capt. Pechell and Sir George Bowyer of Radley Park, who between them owned four and a half

2 MacDermot p.86.

miles of the proposed nine and a half mile track. Abingdon also objected to the line, through the borough Member of Parliament Mr Duffield. Vested interest had ended the project almost before it had been started. The same scheme was revived in 1838 without the Abingdon branch, which was abandoned because the Member of Parliament for the town, Mr Duffield, was opposing it on behalf of the town authorities with all means at his disposal. This latest proposal, however, was defeated again in the Lords, this time by University opposition brought to bear through their Chancellor, the Duke of Wellington, who among other things said railways were bad "because they encouraged the lower classes to move about."

Another abortive effort in 1840 left Oxford with Steventon as a station, but eight road-coaches ran daily, taking ninety minutes, at a fare of 3s (15p). In 1842 77,567 passengers and 12,620 tons of goods were dealt with at Steventon and the village was regarded by Great Western authorities as an important first-class station, so much so that the company consolidated its London and Bristol management committees at Steventon, and in 1841 made it the organising centre of the Great Western Railway. In July 1842, the first meeting of directors was held there and in January 1843 took place what proved to be the last, for the company after six months at Steventon decided to transfer all its operations to Paddington. By this time Oxford passengers began to feel the inconvenience of having no railway. The 1838 project was revived despite George Stephenson's scheme for a line to run from Moulsford through Wallingford to Magdalen Bridge, but a Bill in the 1843 Parliamentary Session provided for a line from Didcot to "a certain field belonging to Brasenose College or west of Abingdon Turnpike road in the Liberty of Grand Pont and Parish of St. Aldate in the City of Oxford."

To preserve Univesity discipline the company provided that the Vice-Chancellor, Proctors, Heads of Houses, and University Marshall should have free access to the station at all train departure times to ensure no junior members travelled. The University forbade the company to convey such members below the degree of M.A. or B.C.L. under the penalty of £5 for each offence. The Royal Assent was given to the Bill in April 1843 and the line was completed in early June a year later.

The Oxford line was put into service on June 12th 1844, and the same day a junction station came into use at Didcot — a building at that time with a large over-all roof, which was burnt down in March 1885. The Didcot to Newbury line came in 1882 and was much favoured by Lord Wantage who saw it as linking various of his farms on the southern side of the Lockinge Estate. It also gave access to the rifle ranges at Churn and in both world wars formed an important routeway from the midlands through Oxford on a direct line to Southampton.

From Radley the Abingdon extension was completed in 1856 and opened on June 2nd as a broad gauge line which had been built in under a year by the Abingdon Railway Company, the Great Western undertaking to work it. The Abingdon Railway Company functioned until 1904, when the shareholders were offered £20 of Great Western Railway Co. Ordinary Stock for each £10 holding in the Abingdon company. [3]

So the region's efforts during the railway age were not entirely uneventful, but as a result largely of landowners' personal interests being forcefully expressed, Wallingford, Abingdon, Wantage and Faringdon were kept off the line of the main route, and for some years Oxford was without a railway.

3 Townsend A History of Abingdon p.158.

WAILINGS AT WANTAGE

By one who is subject to the gout

From the station to Wantage an omnibus runs —
  A small one — now pray do not laugh,
When I tell you the fare they charge over there
  Is a 'bob' for two miles and a half . . .

They think bye and bye the rail will come nigh,
  And then at the 'bus they will laugh;
They will ride in good style at a penny a mile
  and no 'bobs' for two miles and a half . . .

(1866)

AND LATER . . .
AN ACTUAL FACT

A curious race has come to pass,
  Between an engine and an ass.
The Wantage Tram, all steam and smoke,
  Was beat by Arthur Hitchcock's moke.

(1923)

The Great Western Railway does not come nearer Wantage Town than the station called Wantage Road. The above amusing lines represent the feeling in Wantage in recent years upon the sluggish light railway connecting the main line to the town.

(The Berkshire Book of Song, Rhymes & Steeple Chimes,
by A. L. Humphreys)

21

The Wantage tramway

Although the Great Western Railway was built through Grove and Challow in 1840, Wantage Road station did not supersede Faringdon Road as the stopping point for Wantage until 1846, and from that year a horse-drawn bus met every train, taking the passengers on to Wantage. The idea of a tramway to replace the bus, mooted about 1874, was eagerly taken up and within two years Wantage became the first place in England to run a steam tramway. Apart from the convenience to passengers and a clear reduction in transport cost for bulky goods such as road-stone, grain, semi-finished metals and timber, a complete change came over the coal trade. Formerly the town was dependent on the Wiltshire and Berkshire canal to bring coal from Somerset and Gloucestershire, but now Midland coal, of higher quality and lower cost, was available.

The initial notice launching the tramway appeared displayed in Wantage announcing: "A meeting of persons favourable to a tramway communication between the town of Wantage and the Wantage Road station of the Great Western Railway will be held at the Town Hall in Wantage on Wednesday, October 22 1873, at half-past three in the afternoon." Lt-Col. Loyd-Lindsay, VC, MP, took the chair and the project was duly agreed to, the necessary initial finance raised and the project started.

Voluminous preliminary work carried through by a town solicitor, Mr. Ormond, resulted in a Provisional Order for the Wantage tramway being settled by the Board of Trade, and in August 1874 it received the Royal Assent. By the following August the two-and-a-half miles of track neared completion, and soon a horse-drawn carriage taking fifteen minutes between the market place and the station was in operation. But while horses plodded down the line experiments took place with Grantham's car, an open-ended and open-roofed steam-operated coach. Initially the Board of Trade refused permission for its use, but by the intercession of Mr. Walmsley (parliamentary agent acting for the tramway company) and Col. Loyd-Lindsay, the Government relented and Parliament authorised the use of steam power in April 1876. Early in its career the Grantham car was involved in two accidents, both on the line near Grove bridge, while in 1880 a head-on crash occurred near the town terminus. Both trams were badly damaged, but fortunately nobody in the crowded coaches was injured.

Between 1880 and the First World War, when steam power had become established, the line expanded and prospered. From 1880 six passenger trains ran daily, and the service was extended until in 1900 the trams carried just under 40,000 passengers. Fares were moderate. In about 1906 from Wantage to Wantage Road cost 6d (2½p), to Grove bridge 2d (1p), and to Oxford Lane 4d (2p). By 1920 market tickets available on Wednesdays and Saturdays cost 1s (5p) between the station and town at a time when the normal single fare was 9d (4p). Combined tram and rail cheap tickets cost 3s 2d (16p) to Oxford and 4s 1d (21p) to Reading. By 1906 the service had reached thirteen trips a day, meeting sixteen stopping trains. The first journey was at 7.05 am, the final at 7.50 pm, but on Saturdays another tram allowed later return to Wantage at 8.30 pm.

A few years earlier a new two-storey office with a terracotta frontage was built on Mill Street and inscribed Wantage Tramway Co. 1904. The manager worked upstairs, while below passengers filed through the booking hall into the terminus.

About this time a plan was evolved to extend the line down to Clark's mill by the Letcombe brook, but eventually only a terminus in the freight yard was built, by the canal-wharf cottages, and goods were carted to the mill. Clark's guaranteed to take six hundred tons of goods a month for ten years, initially at 1s (5p) a ton, but rates were often revised. Besides grain, general cargo came to the lower yard: furniture, road metal for the council, timber and coal for gasworks and merchants.

By 1906 passenger use of the line had risen to 56,180, but it fell again with the onset of war, when, apart from a depletion of trade and wage and cost rises, the town mill closed and passenger fares were forced up. Revenue declined after 1919, and in 1924, by which time the G.W.R. had established a road service between Swindon and Wantage, the rail company agreed to manage passenger, parcels and mail services. By August 1925 fifty years of passenger transport had ended. Now wholly a goods line, the trams handled freight, especially to the mill. From 1929 Mr. P. S. Clark managed the line from his mill office. Now only three trips a day each way coped sufficiently with goods, but in just over ten years the Second World War again saw a period of prosperity in the line and revenues rose sharply, largely due to restrictions on road vehicles. The success of the early war years ended abruptly in 1943, owing partly to United States servicemen who were on Grove airfield. Their transport caused thick mud to cover the track during the 1943-4 winter and services were suspended.

Restarted in February 1944, the line continued until January 1946, when an extra-ordinary general meeting decided to dispose of all assets and liquidate the company. The final phase in the tramway's history came in April 1946, when a letter to *The Times* suggested that a tramway engine should remain in Wantage. Just before nationalization Sir James Milne, of the Great Western, intervened and secured *Shannon* which stood on Wantage Road's down platform, to mark, in Milne's words, "the long association between the tramway company, the town of Wantage and ourselves" — the old Great Western Railway.

ELECTION OF MAYOR AT ABINGDON IN 1835

On Tuesday last the ceremony of Mayor-choosing by the potwallopers of this borough, took place, probably for the last time. W. D. Belcher, Esq. was distinguished on the present occasion by the undivided suffrages of the electors, whom he treated as usual with bread and cheese and beer in the County Hall. Mr. Godfrey was chosen Commoner's Bailiff, also without opposition, and added liberally to the potations furnished by the Mayor elect. Mr. G. Morland was appointed the Mayor's Bailiff. These gentlemen come into office on the 29th instant.

(*Jackson's Oxford Journal*, September 5th, 1835)

22
Local government and Education

The parish, hundred and county were the basic units of rural administration in the late eighteenth and early nineteenth centuries, and since medieval times they had remained largely unchanged. The parish as an ecclesiastical unit was a grouping of population sufficient to form a congregation and developed hand in hand with the manor, for it enabled the Lord of the Manor in a paternal role to offer the parish his patronage.

The hundreds were initially groupings of parishes with a total of one hundred families, and Berkshire consisted of nineteen hundreds. The eight hundreds in north Berkshire were named partly after places, as in Faringdon, Shrivenham, Wantage, Morton and Compton, and comprised the area around these centres. The three remaining hundreds were Ganfield, stretching from Longworth to Stanford-in-the-Vale, Ock, which carved out a crescent of territory from Appleton through Garford, Hanney to Drayton and Long Wittenham, and Hormer which stretched from Abingdon north to Wytham.

Berkshire's nineteen hundreds were presided over by a Sheriff, but the Justices of the Peace, appointed by the Crown, increasingly gained his administrative functions in addition to meeting once a quarter to try criminal offences at Quarter Sessions.

But at a lower level of rural administration the villages came into contact with the parish and its vestry committee, for, as we have seen, this unit levied poor rates and operated poor relief. Further administrative functions fell into different hands, the main roads, for instance, were in the control of the turnpike trustees, but their upkeep was often less than satisfactory.

The middle and later years of the nineteenth century were the great era of local government reform, both nationally and in north Berkshire. To cope with a cholera epidemic temporary local Boards of Health were formed in 1831 with a Central Board of Health to co-ordinate them, and this was one of the first national authorities. It was followed in 1834 by reform of the Poor Law organization where the parishes were formed into Poor Law Unions which coincided with the old hundreds and were made responsible for giving poor relief. The Unions were locally controlled by elected Boards of Guardians and nationally by the Poor Law Commissioners.

Local administration of the boroughs, such places as Abingdon, Wallingford, and Newbury, was re-organized by Municipal Corporation Acts in 1835 and 1882. But it was the onrush of the industrial revolution and increasing urbanization of Britain which led to wholesale change in the third quarter of the century. As a further central body, the Local Government Board was established in 1871 to consider all local government matters. A Public Health Act in 1872 divided the country into urban and rural sanitary areas, the forerunners of Urban and Rural Districts each with their own elected councils. At the same time (1894) the parish system was brought up to date. Previously the Local Government Act of 1888 had created County Boroughs, such as Reading, from the larger towns, and administrative counties from the ancient counties, and established elected councils in these areas.

The local government map of north Berkshire was consequently completed between 1835 and 1894; the Boroughs of Abingdon and Wallingford having been reformed twice within this period, the Urban District of Wantage was formed, and Rural Districts were carved from the hundreds in the country areas surrounding Faringdon, Wantage, Abingdon and Wallingford. In overall control was the Berkshire County Council resulting from the 1888 Act of Parliament.

The historic centre of the area was Abingdon, which held the position of County Town of Berkshire until the much expanded size enabled Reading to take over the function in 1869; consequently Abingdon has a County Hall, County Gaol and County Police Station. The County Gaol overlooks the Thames beside Burford Bridge and was erected in 1811 for £26,000 to house a Court House for the Summer Assize and July County Court Sessions. The October County Sessions were held alternately with Reading. The prison has had several functions and held French prisoners during Napoleonic struggles, but in more recent decades came under the aegis of Abingdon's foremost grain merchant.

Educationally north Berkshire was quite well advanced during the nineteenth century compared to other parts of the county. In the towns several elementary schools were set up by the two charitable societies, namely the *National Society for the Education of the Poor according to the Principles of the Church of England*, and *The British and Foreign School Society*.

The National or Church schools came to be the usual vehicles of education in the local villages and towns, and a National School was established in Abingdon by public subscription in 1824. It was on a site close to St. Helen's church and was designed to hold one hundred and twenty boys and ninety girls. Running costs were met by a weekly contribution from parents of one penny for each child. The second society was set up under non-conformist and whig patronage and worked on the basis of undenominational Bible teaching. Abingdon's British School was built in Ock Street, also in1824; boys were taught on the lower floor and the girls upstairs. An addition allowed infants to be taken in 1852 and the school roll in 1860 accounted for one hundred and twenty boys and two hundred girls.

There were further National Schools at Wallingford, Wantage and Faringdon. The Wallingford school was in Castle Street from 1828 and accommodated ninety boys and forty girls; Wantage National School was in Back Street and in 1860 took one hundred and twenty boys at three-farthings a week each. Girls were taken on the same premises, eighty-seven of them at one penny a week, while an infants' school in the same building catered for a further one hundred and twelve pupils.

Faringdon National School was established in 1825 for one hundred and twenty boys, but the British School did not come until 1853 and had a capacity of one hundred and forty places, although in 1860 it had only sixty-four pupils on the books.

Superimposed on the local pattern of National and British Schools were village elementary schools of ancient foundation at Appleton, Uffington, Harwell, Blewbury, Childrey [1] and Chaddleworth, with Belcher's School and Provost's School both at Abingdon. Appleton School, founded by Sir Richard Fettiplace in 1604, had endowments added by Thomas Lane in 1709 to teach six boys in learning, good manners and the three R's. Uffington School, coupled with Woolstone, dates from 1640 and, endowed with land and property in the village, kept a schoolmaster charged with teaching the three R's to twelve boys from Uffington and six from Woolstone. The Charity Commissioners in 1896 spent the endowment income, but the Board of Education later borrowed money on the security of the endowment to improve the school.

William Malthus' School at Blewbury was formed in 1700. In the early nineteenth century sixty children were taught by a master paid £50 a year, and a mistress paid £20 a year.[2] Provost's School in Abingdon taught eleven boys reading, writing and arithmetic; they were also clothed and apprenticed at fourteen if desired, while Belcher's School taught fifteen poor boys to read English. In addition to the pattern of schools already developed, the Education Act of 1870 fostered the Church Schools and introduced Board Schools to fill gaps in the system, to be paid for out of the rates and managed by elected School Boards. The public system of education remained much the same until Arthur Balfour's Education Act of 1902 abolished the school boards and gave the elected County Councils, and some large Borough Councils, responsibility for primary and secondary education.

1 See WHC pp.83-4.
2 See WHC pp.152-3.

The three ancient Grammar Schools at Wantage, Wallingford and Abingdon catered for a different market and provided an academic secondary education. Wallingford Grammar School originated in Cross House. Wantage Grammar School stood beside the parish church but by 1832 had declined, having only one scholar. It was decided to revive the school as a memorial of King Alfred's millenary in 1849 and a new King Alfred's School was built in the Portway in 1850 to designs of William Butterfield.

Abingdon School is pre-Norman in origin, and one of the oldest foundations in England. Re-founded in 1563 by John Roysse a mercer of London, it had a schoolroom measuring sixty-three feet long, held sixty-three scholars and was re-endowed in the sixty-third year of John Roysse's life. Moving to its present site adjoining Albert Park in 1870, the school has been much extended and now houses six hundred and thirty pupils, exactly ten times John Roysse's original endowment. In the late eighteenth and nineteenth centuries the school produced numerous distinguished men. Viscount Tracey became Warden of All Souls, Thomas Dudley Fosbrook was a well-known antiquarian, Dr. William Newcome became Archbishop of Armagh and Dr. William Collinson Sawyer was Bishop of Grafton and Armidale in New South Wales. In addition the school produced a succession of Masters of Pembroke College, Oxford, for the College was established by Thomas Tesdale of Abingdon and William Wightwick of East Ilsley as a hall specifically for scholars from Abingdon School; Abingdonian Masters include Dr. William Adams (1775-89), William Sergrove (1789-96), Dr. John Smyth (1796-1809) and Dr. George Hall (1809-43) who was also Vice-Chancellor for four years from 1820.

In the later Victorian period there was a national emphasis on establishing boarding and day schools for children of the wealthier classes. This was not only associated with the accumulation of wealth resulting from business success, but also with the development of the railway system which put the countryside in reach of the towns. Among these schools is St. Peter's College, Radley, which in 1847 was set up by the Rev. William Sewell, Fellow of Exeter College, in Radley Hall, for long the home of the Bowyer family. On the other side of the area Bradfield College was founded by the Rev. Thomas Stevens, Lord of the Manor and Rector of Bradfield, in 1850. At Wantage St. Mary's School was set up in 1874 as a girls' boarding school and as the teaching wing of the Wantage Order of St. Mary the Virgin, and was followed by St. Katherine's School in 1897. The School of St. Helen and St. Katherine for girls at Abingdon dates from 1902 and was formed by merging St. Katherine's which moved from Wantage with St. Helen's School Abingdon.

The following two chapters deal with three men who influenced the Vale of White Horse: George Street's legacy is visible in the churches and buildings he designed; the impact of Lord Wantage is quite clear at Ardington and Lockinge, on the Lockinge estate and in the buildings of Wantage. One of Martin Tupper's cherished intentions was brought to fruition by Lord Wantage twenty-eight years after Tupper had led the Wantage celebration of the thousandth anniversary of King Alfred's birth, in the erection of a statue to the King.

23

George Street, distinguished church architect

The Vale is richly endowed with numerous early village churches, and during the Victorian era many of them underwent restoration, and a large number of new churches were erected, either as fresh structures or to replace a building which had gone before. George Edmund Street, who came to live at Wantage early in 1850, made a decisive contribution to the ecclesiastical and educational buildings of the area. He was a young Tractarian architect and exponent of the gothic style. It was in designing churches that some of his genius became apparent and was fostered by a close association with the pre-raphaelites. William Morris was Street's pupil; he had the Rosettis, Ford Madox-Brown and Burne Jones among his closest friends, gathering from them notable inspiration for his architectural work.

George Street came to Wantage through the Ecclesiological Society's secretary, Benjamin Webb, who recommended him to the Rev. William Butler, vicar of Wantage. Butler employed Street to design a new vicarage, but in turn introduced him to Bishop Wilberforce of Oxford who appointed Street honorary diocesan architect. Under the lead of Wilberforce, Street's artistic influence was widely felt throughout the diocese. Following Butler's expansive plans, Street drew designs for St Michael's and the Wantage Retreat House, and in 1854 for the Convent of the Wantage Order; he built a school opposite the parish church, and reputedly drew reconstruction designs for the red-brick, timber-framed shops beside the town hall in Wantage market place.

Commissions throughout the Vale came increasingly easily. He restored Uffington church; in local stone built Stanford-in-the-Vale's school; in 1856 he designed East Hanney church in a simple nave and chancel form. Of this building a commentator noted that it was remarkable for its date, "just a barn with a few irregularly spaced windows, entirely different from the Puginist style of nave and chancel chapel".

East Challow school was built in 1852 and, as at St Michael's and the Wantage Convent, his method of incorporating chimney stacks as integral parts of the building's design is easily seen; initially the stacks acted as buttresses, then narrowed into slender pillars. Restoring Coleshill church and designing Denchworth school came in 1852, while the following year he restored the inside of Denchworth church.

Of all the villages in the Vale countryside, Brightwalton probably owes most to Street. He designed the church and school, built in 1863, and the vicarage, erected in 1877. Fawley church — an almost perfect example of Street's style — came in 1866; soon after he built Eastbury and Watchfield churches. He toured continental cities frequently to examine major French and German gothic cathedrals, and to widen his experience of design, but following his tour of 1851 he moved from Wantage, setting himself up in Beaumont Street, Oxford, from where he completed two of his most important local works, Bloxham School and the design for Cuddesdon Theological College. As Street widened his horizons, later architectural triumphs occurred elsewhere, and by now he was acting as diocesan architect not only to Oxford, but to Ripon, York and Winchester. He was called upon to plan restoration of Carlisle cathedral, York Minster and Salisbury cathedral. He also planned and saw completed the rebuilding of Bristol cathedral's nave.

Towards the end of Street's career his standing alongside Scott as a great champion of gothic architecture was becoming undisputed. His career culminated in producing the winning design for the new Law Courts at the western end of Fleet Street in London. He made over three thousand drawings before completing the plan, and had so much difficulty that it was feared the work was too great for him. He died in 1881, a year before the building was finished, and was buried in the nave of Westminster Abbey among the famous of the land.

Tupperian, a. adj. Of, belonging to, or in the style of Martin F Tupper's Proverbial Philosophy (1838-42) **b.** An admirer of Tupper. So Tupperish a., Tupperism, Tupperize.

(The Oxford English Dictionary)

24

Martin Tupper and
Lord Wantage

There were countless red-letter days in nineteenth-century north Berkshire. One occurred late in October 1849 at Wantage when Martin Tupper, a well connected Victorian do-gooder, arranged the celebration of the thousandth anniversary of King Alfred's birth. Tupper, a typical Victorian, passed to Oxford where at Christ Church he came into contact with numerous people who were to help him later in life. Among them were Lord Lincoln (later Duke of Newcastle), W. E. Gladstone, both Henry Liddell and Robert Scott (of Greek-English dictionary fame), and Charles Canning, a future Governor-General of India.

Lifelong friendship with Gladstone was based upon a common and deep interest in church affairs, and it was partly through this connection that Tupper was elected a Fellow of the Royal Society. The publication of his *Proverbial Philosophy* also helped, a "book of thoughts and arguments originally treated by Martin F. Tupper, Esq. M.A."

During the early portion of 1849 Martin Tupper championed two major causes which were close to his heart: the furthering of a literary magazine *The Anglo-Saxon*, and organizing the thousandth anniversary of King Alfred's birth. In *The Anglo-Saxon*, Tupper thumped the drum for the Wantage Alfred celebration. Writing of the King as "the father of Anglo-Saxon greatness", Tupper had always been an admirer of King Alfred, and his celebration prospectus formed a "call to the good and great of the Anglo-Saxon race" for financial support to satisfy his venture. Copies were sent to the Dukes of Wellington, Northumberland and Richmond, Lord Ashley, Benjamin

Disraeli, Lord John Russell, and Sir Robert Peel. Not too surprisingly just three replied — Ashley, Richmond and Peel.

A much smaller local committee was formed by John Hughes at Donnington Priory comprising the Rev. W. J. Butler (Vicar of Wantage), Dr J. A. Groves of Bampton (biographer of King Alfred) and W. J. Evelyn of Wootton. They attempted to enthuse the local gentry, but just as the original group had rebuffed Tupper, so too the local big-wigs rejected Tupper's committee. It was only after the Lord Mayor had refused a public dinner in London's Guildhall that Tupper decided that the celebration, if it was to take place at all, should be entirely centred on Wantage.

Gradually the tide began to turn and the persuasive charm of Dr Groves and Martin Tupper helped to win over the local gentry one by one. First came Charles Eyston of East Hendred, who agreed to help the committee; then Philip Pusey of Pusey House subscribed £10 for a statue of Alfred to be built in Wantage.

Careful plans were laid, and the great day, Thursday October 29 1849, dawned. "A great and unprecedented honour" had been thrust upon Wantage, proclaimed a Tupper poster displayed in the town. Flags, banners and bunting went up in the streets, and Wantage rose to the occasion. Bands paraded, a fair was set up in a field outside the town towards Grove, an ox gently roasted in the market place, turned by one of Mr. Charles Hart's famous Wantage steam engines, while at the far end of the square townsfolk scrambled up a greasy pole to win a leg of mutton.

The Morning Post said: "the day was observed by all parties as a public holiday, and business was universally suspended". The Rev. William Butler conducted divine service in the parish church. A procession moved to the market singing Tupper's jubilee song, *Today is the Day of a Thousand Years*, and Major Bell, a hired professional lecturer, spoke from the town hall about the Wantage king. Later at King Alfred's well, the Rev. F. Reyroux spoke of Alfred, and he was in turn followed by the Duke of Richmond, who, according to *The Morning Post*, spoke on the same subject and at considerable length.

The town poor received roast meat from the ox and one hundred jubilee medals were distributed. With blue ribbands attached, they bore Alfred's effigy. Additional copies in gold, silver, bronze or white metal were sold at varying prices. Elsewhere, a special dinner for one hundred gentlemen took place at the King Alfred's Head, and Philip Pusey brought the famous Pusey Horn, from which the toast was drunk, proposed by Tupper, to the Anglo-Saxon race all over the world. The great day concluded with a grand ball in the town hall.

Although no statue was built, permanent results came from the Alfred celebration, for a resolution was passed at the dinner that the Elizabethan grammar school, at the time in a sad state of decay, should be revived as King Alfred's College; a mechanics institute was to be founded; and Dr Groves announced the impending publication of his *Life of Alfred. The Morning Post* noted that in all some 20,000 people came to the town's celebration and that there was no drunkenness, thieving or fighting. For a town once so rough that it was widely known as Black Wantage, this was indeed a notable achievement.

Wantage folk waited for twenty-eight years for her statue of King Alfred, towards which Philip Pusey had subscribed £10 in 1849, and they waited too for another benefactor, as neither Tupper nor Pusey fulfilled the pledge to erect a statue.

The year was 1877 and the benefactor was the future Lord Wantage. On that late July morning, flags, bunting, and triumphal arches once again spanned the roadways, while every shop around the market place was brightly decorated. A whole host of country people trooped into town by all manner of transport, on foot from Charlton and Challow, by pony-trap from the downland villages, while Grove people paid their sixpence from Oxford Lane and came in style on the recently opened tramway. The occasion was the visit of the Prince of Wales and Princess Alexandra of Denmark, to unveil the statue of King Alfred in the market place. The statue was presented to the town by Colonel Loyd-Lindsay, MP, of Lockinge, and throughout the weekend of the visit the Prince and his wife stayed at Lockinge House.

As we have seen, the millenary celebration of Alfred's birth came and went in 1849 but still no permanent monument to the King had been erected, and it was left to the imagination of a local member of parliament to commission a statue to stand in the market place of Wantage amid the Berkshire countryside which was so deeply associated with the struggles of Wessex and the King.

Count Gleichen, Prince Victor of Hohenlohe-Langenburg, was invited to prepare the design. Eventually the figure arrived and was erected; first the granite steps, then the base, finally the statue itself — eight feet high and chiselled in white marble from Sicily. Everyone passing through the town knows that bearded face of Alfred. One hand clutches a scroll representing the scholar, teacher and writer in him. A plaque records the measure of his greatness: "Alfred found learning dead and he restored it, education neglected and he revived it, the laws powerless and he gave them force, the church debased and he raised it, the land ravaged by a fearful enemy from which he delivered it. Alfred's name shall live as long as mankind shall respect the past." The facial likeness is said to be that of Lord Wantage himself.

The Royal party travelled to Wantage Road Station in a special train of saloon coaches containing every fussy Victorian trimming. Colonel Loyd-Lindsay along with the Lord Lieutenant of Berkshire, the Earl of Abingdon (High Sheriff of the County), the Bishop of Oxford and two other local members of parliament, greeted the guests, and carriages took the party to town, escorted by a troop of the Berkshire Yeomanry.

At the market place the Prince took his seat on a raised platform directly facing the statue, which was covered by a blue and white cloth. The band of the Grenadiers struck up, played the national anthem and the proceedings started. On behalf of a throng of townsfolk in the market place, Mr H. de Vitre read an address of welcome to the visitors from an illuminated scroll, and accepted the statue on behalf of the townspeople. The Prince replied in suitably brief and complimentary terms; then came the presentations.

As a token of his visit the Prince planted a lime tree and unveiled the statue. The Grenadiers' band played, the Wantage Rifle Volunteers presented arms, the Royal party re-mounted their coaches, and Wantage attempted to return to normal life. For the remainder of that weekend the centre of excitement moved to Lockinge, and although rain spoilt much of the Wantage ceremony, it failed completely to dampen spirits. Conditions at Lockinge were more congenial for merry-making: everything took place under cover. During Saturday afternoon a garden party was forced inside a marquee by persistent rain, but the chatter continued unabated and the company was entertained by a skilful group of Indian jugglers. That evening the whole visit was rounded off by a dinner party given for the Prince in Lockinge House at which over eighty guests from all over Berkshire were present. One doubts whether the Wantage area has since seen an event so lavish in its proportions.

As a distinguished soldier, holder of the Victoria Cross, a politician of some merit, and an enterprising landowner, Robert Lindsay, first Baron Wantage of Lockinge, was the most distinguished person living in late-nineteenth-century north Berkshire, and by building the King Alfred Statue brought to fruition the task Martin Tupper had started. Born in 1832, the son of General James Lindsay, he passed from Eton to the Scots Guards as a subaltern for a military career, short but noteworthy. Quickly drafted to the Crimea, he carried the Queen's Colour at the Battle of Alma. Following a second gallant role at the Battle of Inkerman, Lindsay was posted aide-de-camp to Sir James Simpson, but the same year left that appointment to be regimental adjutant. It was after the war, while Lindsay instructed musketry at the new Hythe School of Musketry, that he was Gazetted one of the first recipients of the Victoria Cross with double commendations for services at Alma and Inkerman. The same year, after appointment as Equerry to the Prince of Wales, Lindsay married Harriet

Loyd, daughter of Lord Overstone, and assumed the name Loyd-Lindsay. He resigned from the army in the rank of lieutenant-colonel and farmed the Lockinge Estate which had been given to the couple as a wedding present by Lord Overstone.

As a farmer and landowner Robert Loyd-Lindsay was particularly noted in north Berkshire. He rebuilt and extended Ardington and Lockinge as model villages, established a co-operative selling good quality food at moderate prices and became one of southern England's late-nineteenth-century agricultural pioneers. During the great agricultural slump of the 1870's resulting largely from cheap wheat production in the United States, Loyd-Lindsay moved land from wheat cultivation to more profitable barley growing, and when tenant farmers were in financial trouble, he with characteristic generosity gave them some degree of rent abatement. So far as actual farming techniques were concerned, he pioneered the use of basic slag on thin downland soils, established a number of Shire Horse teams, and in Grove Park maintained one of Berkshire's largest herds of Hereford cattle.

He also pioneered the Volunteer Movement in Britain — an achievement recalled by the Volunteer inn at Wantage Road Station on the edge of the estate at Grove Park — and in 1860 was promoted to Colonel commanding the county detachment. With reorganization in 1888 he was appointed Brigadier-General in charge of the Home Counties Brigade. Apart from enthusiasm for a mounted element in the Volunteers, he was an expert shot, and as chairman of the National Rifle Association founded Bisley's Loyd-Lindsay Prize.

The House of Commons career of this north Berkshire landowner continued for twenty years after his election as the County Member in 1865. Benjamin Disraeli chose him as Financial Secretary to the War Office, and with the outbreak of the Franco-Prussian war Loyd-Lindsay took steps to found the National Society for aid to the sick and wounded, which developed into the Red Cross Aid Society. As its chairman he visited the war front in France — was entertained by the Prussians at their headquarters in Versailles — then managed to penetrate the besieged city of Paris. Only protracted illness prevented him sailing for South Africa to direct the Red Cross Aid Society in the Boer War. During later life two distinctions were conferred on Loyd-Lindsay. On the twenty-first anniversary of the Volunteer Corps he became Knight Commander of the Order of the Bath; four years later in 1885 he was appointed Lord Lieutenant of Berkshire and was then raised to the Barony as Lord Wantage of Lockinge.

Beside receiving national honours Lord Wantage had a more direct personal influence upon north Berkshire. The tall marble column on the Ridgeway above Lockinge was raised as a memorial soon after his death in 1901. He extended the estate to over seven thousand acres, and took a personal interest in launching the tramway to Wantage Road Station, despite the fact that his predecessors at Lockinge were instrumental in diverting the Great Western Railway away from Wantage and off the estate. As we have already seen, he also negotiated the erection of Count Gleichen's statue of King Alfred in Wantage market place, presented the site for a town hall, helping financially with its building, and gave a collection of paintings for the Victoria Cross Gallery. But probably Lord Wantage's greatest service to the town occurred when he bought and extended the ailing Wantage Iron Works at the foot of Chain hill, for it faced financial disaster; his purchase saved numerous jobs and secured one of the mainstays of the Wantage economy.

ON THE ROAD FROM GOOSEY TO WEST HANNEY, 1908

Few vehicles haunt the lonely road except milk-carts bound for the station, and gipsy vans that on their way to fresh camping places leave their mark behind them in a patch of black ashes at each halt. Wayside cottages are rare, and the only hint of the sleepy hamlets to right and left is supplied by the 'handingposts' that bear their names.

(*Islands of the Vale* by Eleanor Hayden)

25

Prelude to the twentieth century

Through the closing years of the nineteenth century and first decade of the twentieth, north Berkshire was in a state of enterprise, mobility and change. When Victoria came to the throne in 1837 the area was in many respects much the same as it had been in early Georgian times. By Queen Victoria's Jubilee the Berkshire Vale was fast catching up with the rapid industrial and commercial progress that coal, steel, cotton, the canal system and railway network had brought to northern and midland England in previous decades. Berkshire was destined to remain predominantly agricultural, but developments in industrial England slowly rippled outwards, and to some extent foreshadowed changes which took place in our region after the Great War.

It was in the towns that expansion was greatest; this was partly related to increased civic and religious consciousness. At Abingdon the distinctive suburb in the park, which was open cornland before 1864, became the focal point of a new and typically Victorian urban development to some extent paralleling the extension of north Oxford. Albert Park, as it was called, commemorated the Prince Consort who had died in 1861; a monument to him was unveiled with some ceremony in 1865. Abingdon market place too was in a state of redevelopment. The Queen's Arms gave way to the Queen's Hotel in 1864. Abingdon School moved out of the town centre to a new site adjoining Albert Park in 1870. The Corn Exchange and present National Westminster Bank building came in 1886, Queen Victoria's statue appeared in 1887, and the Free Library in High Street was opened in 1896.

The period saw the erection of three new ecclesiastical buildings: the Congregational Chapel in the Square (1862), St Michael's Church (1867) in Park Road, designed by Sir G. G. Scott, and Trinity Methodist Church, also in Park Road (1875). Wantage, and Wallingford to a lesser degree, experienced a late Victorian development. During these years the original buildings of the Wantage Sisterhood designed by George Street in 1856 were much added to and altered. A new chapel came in 1887. Additions were made to St Michael's Retreat House in 1888. St Mary's School was completed in 1875, a chapel by C. E. Ponting opened in 1899, and considerably extended in 1900. St Katherine's School in Ormond Road was opened in 1897; other buildings included the Town Hall, Victoria Cross Gallery and office of the Wantage Tramway Company.

This substantial development was not generally echoed in the Berkshire villages, which were almost as remote in 1900 as they had been throughout the previous century. Roads, in most places still unsealed, saw increasing traffic by horse, cart, waggon, pony-trap, and eventually traction engine between the various villages and the towns; it was not until the 1920's that the motor vehicle became at all common, but nevertheless this gradual change in the form of traffic served to link indissolubly the economy of the village and town. Village self-sufficiency eventually gave way to a rural-urban interdependence, centred initially upon the market towns of Wantage, Wallingford, Faringdon, Newbury and Abingdon, but later upon Oxford, Reading and, in the west of the Vale, Swindon.

Increased importance of the towns in the local economy was related not only to improved access but also to their offering opportunities for employment. At Oxford the cycle shop belonging to William Morris, opened in 1893, developed into the Nuffield Organization and the British Leyland Motor Corporation of today. The first Morris car was produced in 1913 in Oxford, but not until after the Great War did industrial development get underway and eventually spread from Cowley to Birmingham, Coventry and Abingdon.

At Swindon the major development was a large complex of railway engineering workshops — as chance would have it, a development turned down by both Oxford and Abingdon. But it did impinge upon the area, providing employment in the western Vale.

Although industrial development began to make selective inroads into the area, using electricity rather than coal for power, agriculture and associated industries such as milling and brewing were still overridingly important in the local economy and remained relatively prosperous until after the Great War. A measure of the changed emphasis which arose during the nineteenth century can be seen in population figures quoted in table 1 and comment not just on population increase, but on a relative change between town and countryside. Between 1801 and 1901 Abingdon's population rose from 4,683 to 6,689; Reading's from 9,742 to 59,018, and Oxford's from 12,279 to 49,336. Rural centres increased by smaller proportions, and remote villages such as East Ilsley, East Hendred and Lambourn remained virtually static or suffered a decrease.

The three revolutions mentioned in the first chapter, namely the agricultural, industrial and transport revolutions, in time extended from before the eighteenth century through to the nineteenth century, and prepared the way for the fourth sequence of change, the scientific and technological revolution of the twentieth century. Midland and northern England had taken the lead in the industrial revolution and in the early stages of the transport revolution; the fourth revolution put north Berkshire into the forefront of change. Fostered by the proximity of Oxford University, and to a lesser extent Reading University, and by the ease of access to London, a number of important centres of scientific research were established in the vicinity. To a disused airfield on the Berkshire Downs above Harwell came the Atomic Energy Research Establishment, at Aldermaston was set up the Atomic Weapons Research Establishment, the Culham Laboratories were formed on another disused airfield between

Abingdon and Dorchester, and Letcombe Regis and Compton have laboratories of the Agricultural Research Council.

BIBLIOGRAPHY

GENERAL BOOKS
A number of economic histories cover the period 1780 to 1914 in a graphically descriptive manner, and offer a splendid background of economic and social activity to the changes that were taking place in The Vale of the White Horse.

Great Britain from Adam Smith to the Present Day —
  C. R. Fay (1964)
Britain Yesterday and Today — W. M. Stern (1966)
A History of Economic Change in England 1880-1939 —
  R. S. Sayers (1967)

BOOKS ABOUT THE VALE OF THE WHITE HORSE
Additionally, numerous books and pamphlets cover specific topics of relevance to the Vale between 1780 and 1914 dealt with in this book.

A General View of the Agriculture of Berkshire — William
  Mavor (1809)
Letter to the tenants of Philip Pusey Esq, MP for Berkshire
  — John Morton (1838)
The Scouring of the White Horse — Thomas Hughes (1859)
Memoir of George Edmund Street RA — Arthur Edmund
  Street (1888)
Jethro Tull 1674-1740: His Life and Teaching — A. F.
  Cathcart (3rd Earl) (1891)
Philip Pusey 1799-1855 — Sir Ernest Clarke (1900)
A History of the Old Berkshire Hunt from 1760 to 1904 —
  F. C. Loder-Symonds (1905)
Berkshire Sport: MS notes in Reading Public Library —
  P. H. Ditchfield (1905)
Memoir of Lord Wantage — Harriet, Lady Wantage (1907)
News of a Country Town (Abingdon) — James Townshend
  (1914)
The Icknield Way — Edward Thomas (1916)
Rural Industries around Oxford — K. S. Woods (1921)
History of the Great Western Railway. Volumes 1 & 2 —
  E. T. MacDermot (1927) Volume 3 — O. S. Nock (1969)
The Oxford Region — A scientific and historical survey —
  A. F. Martin & R. W. Steel (Editors) (1954)

The Canals of Southern England (1955) and The Canals of South and South-east England — E. C. R. Hadfield (1969)

The Wantage Tramway — S. H. Pearce Higgins (1958)

Estate Villages — M. A. Havinden (1966) (Lockinge Estate)

The Oxford & Newbury Area — P. D. Wood (1968)

Victorian Wantage (1968) & Black Wantage — Kathleen Philip (1971)

Swinford Toll Bridge 1769-1969 — E. de Villiers (1969)

Sickle to Combine. A review of harvest techniques from 1800 to the present day — E. J. T. Collins (1969)

Digest of Directories: Uffington 1847-1907 — John E. Little (1970)

The Upper Thames — J. R. L. Anderson (1970)

The Wilts & Berks Canal — L. J. Dalby (1971)

The White Horse Country — Nigel Hammond (1972)

MAPS

A Topographical Survey of the County of Berkshire — John Rocque (1761)

The Tithe Map of West Hanney — 1844 (Bodleian Library Map Room)

First edition of the one-inch Ordnance Survey, Oxford sheet (70) — 1830

Current edition of the one-inch Ordnance Survey, Oxford & Newbury sheet (158) which will be superseded in due course by the Metric edition on which The Vale of White Horse will be covered by sheets 164 and 174. Ordnance survey 1:25,000 sheets cover the Vale as follows:

Oxford (West)	SP 40	Abingdon	SU 49
Stanford-in-the-Vale	SU 39	Faringdon	SU 29
Blewbury	SU 58	Harwell	SU 48
Lambourn Downs	SU 38	Shrivenham	SU 28

TABLE 1 Population of selected Berkshire towns and villages in 1801, 1851 and 1901

	1801	1851	1901
Abingdon	4,683	6,848	6,689
Buckland	727	987	665
Drayton	484	505	529
East Hendred	683	949	748
East Ilsley	512	750	482
Faringdon	2,153	3,678	3,120
Farnborough	213	224	113
Hungerford	1,987	2,696	2,364
Lambourn	2,045	2,577	2,071
Newbury	4,275	6,574	6,983
Reading	9,742	21,456	59,018
Uffington	432	674	526
Wallingford	1,744	2,864	2,829
Wantage	2,339	3,056	3,766
Oxford	12,279	27,848	49,336

For a fuller account of Berkshire population see *The Victoria County History* Vol.II, pp.234-243

TABLE 2   Key to landholdings on the West Hanney Tithe Map 1844

Number	Type or name	Owner and occupier (C)
34,35	Croft	Thomas Ensworth
36,37	Barns, close and orchard	Thomas Ensworth
38	Morland's close	Thomas Ensworth
39	Orchard	Thomas Ensworth
40	Cottage & garden	Thomas Ensworth
41	Cottage & garden	Esther Wicks
42	Cottage & garden	James Harris
43	Cottage & garden	Widow Harris
44	Close of pasture	William Frogley
45	House & garden	William Cox
46	Homestead	Thomas Godfrey
47	Homestead & orchard	John Kimber
48	Cottages, barn & close of pasture	James and William Monk
49	Cottage & garden	? Smith
50	Garden	W. C. Badcock/James and William Monk (C)
51	House & garden	William Wicks
52,53	Homestead & orchard	John Aldworth/Thomas Godfrey (C)
54	Homestead & orchard	Captain John Holmes
55	Butt's Piece	
56	Rickyard	
57	Orchard	William Aldworth/R. Robins (C)
58	Homestead	
59	Churchyard	
60	Homestead	The Rev. H. R. Barker
100	Cherry orchard	W. C. Badcock/James and William Monks (C)
61	House & premises	Salisbury Cathedral/J. Ensworth (leasee)
62	Cottage & garden	Henry Hearman
63	Cottage & garden	Thomas Godfrey
64	Cottage & garden	James Jones
65,66	Homestead & orchard	Mary Dunsdon
68	Barns & yard	William Aldworth/William Frogley (C)
67	Cottage and gardens	The parish
69	Homestead & orchard	Capt. John Holmes
70	Cottage & garden	Henry Robins
71,72	Cottage, house, garden and premises	Richard Wise
73	Homestead & orchard	Richard Wise
74	Close of pasture	William Aldworth/William Frogley (C)

75	? Mead	
76,77	Matt Furlong, cottage	W. and J. Monk
78	Garden	Thomas Ensworth
79	Cottage & garden	Rachael Robins
80,81	Cottages & gardens	Thomas Ensworth
82	Close	Richard Wise
83	Homestead & orchard	Charles Harris
84	Cottage & orchard	W. & J. Monk
85	Homestead & orchard	W. & J. Monk
86	Cottage & garden	Thomas Godfrey
87	Cottages & gardens	W. & J. Monk
88	Cottage & garden	Charles Harris
89	Cottage & garden	John Stallard
90	Cottage & gardens	Thomas Higgs
91	House & garden	Charles Harris
92,93	Cottage, garden, close	Thomas Godfrey
94	Orchard	W. & J. Monk
95	Homestead & orchard	Charles Harris & Henry Robins
96	House & premises	Thomas Godfrey
97	Homestead	William Aldworth/William Frogley (C)
98	Close	W. & J. Monk
99	Homestead	Thomas King/Richard Wise (C)
101	Cottage & garden	William Wicks
102	House & garden	The Vicar of Buckland
103,104	Two orchards	Thomas Ensworth
105	Homestead & close	W. C. Badcock/W. & J. Monk
106	Cottage & gardens	The Parish
107	Homestead & orchard	Deborah Harris
108	Close	Thomas Godfrey
109	Homestead & close	Captain John Holmes
110	Close of pasture	

TABLE 3   Market days in Berkshire 1815

Monday	Tuesday	Wednesday	Thursday	Friday	Saturday
Abingdon[1]	Faringdon	Hungerford	Newbury	Abingdon[2]	Reading[1]
	Wokingham	Ilsley		Lambourn	Wantage
	Wallingford[2]	Maidenhead		Wallingford[1]	Windsor[1]
		Reading[2]			
		Windsor[2]			

Where towns possessed more than one market each week, the number against the town indicates the order of importance. Often the second market was a time for settlement of bargains struck at the first market, but at Reading and Windsor the two market days saw trade in different commodities. For instance Windsor Saturday market was a well-attended pitched grain-sale with plentiful provisions; the Wednesday market traded solely in eggs, butter, poultry and fruit. Monday market in Abingdon (1811) sold much grain by sample, sheep, poultry, pigs, cattle, and butter; the Friday market was for the delivery of grain sold on the previous Monday, but also sold butter.

TABLE 4 Distribution of Berkshire Town Fairs 1815

January					
February	Reading (2)	Faringdon (13)			
March	Wantage	Abingdon (First Monday in Lent)	Ilsley (26)		Wokingham
April	Wallingford (Tuesday before Easter)	Windsor	Faringdon (Whit Tuesday)	Maidenhead (Whit Wednesday)	Hungerford
May	Lambourn (1)	Wantage	Abingdon (6)		
June	Wokingham (11)	Abingdon (2)	Wallingford (24)		
July	Newbury (5) Windsor (5)	Wantage (18)	Reading (24)		
August	Abingdon (5)	Hungerford (10)	Ilsley (26)		
September	Newbury (4)	Abingdon (1)	Reading (21) Wallingford (21) Wokingham (21)	Maidenhead (29) Abingdon (Old Michaelmas)	
October	Lambourn (4) Hungerford Wantage (17)	Newbury (10) Faringdon (18)	Windsor (25) Faringdon (28)	Ilsley (All Hallows)	
November	Wokingham (2) Newbury (8)		Maidenhead (3)		
December	Lambourn (4)	Abingdon (11)	Wallingford (17)		

Numbers refer to the approximate date when the fair took place; where the date is not known, the fair is placed in the correct relationship to other fairs during that month.

TABLE 5   Distribution of Berkshire Village Fairs 1815

ALDERMASTON (2)	May 6, July 7
BRACKNELL (3)	April 25, August 22, October 1
COOKHAM (2)	May 16, October 11
EAST HAGBOURNE (1)	Thursday before October 11
EAST HENDRED (1)	May, October 11
FINCHAMPSTEAD (1)	First Wednesday in April
HARWELL (1)	Horse fair
STRATFIELD MORTIMER (2)	April 27, November 6
NEWBRIDGE (2)	March 31, September 28
STANFORD-IN-THE-VALE (1)	End of July
SUTTON COURTENAY (1)	Corpus Christi
SWALLOWFIELD (1)	July 9
THATCHAM (2)	Second Tuesday after Easter week First Tuesday after September 29
TWYFORD (2)	July 26, October 11
WADLEY (near Faringdon) (1)	April 6
WALTHAM ST LAWRENCE (1)	August 11 (pleasure and cattle)
YATTENDON (1)	October 13

161

Rabbits 49
Rocque, John 152
Radcot 106, 110
Radley 9, 29, 33, 47, 118, 120
Radnor, Earl of 35
Radway & Co, engineers 22
Railways 89, 116-27, 142
Reading 60, 71, 76, 89, 116
Rents 10-11, 39
Revels 79
Ridgeway 105, 145
Roads 7, 102-7, 119, 151
Rope 54, 62, 112
Rotations 10
Roysse, John 133
Rye Farm 106

Sacking 53
Salt 66
Saxton, Sir Charles 9
Schools
    Abingdon 133, 147
    Bradfield 134
    British 131
    Endowed 132
    National 131, 136
    Radley 133
    St. Mary's 134
    St Helen & St. Katherine 134
Scott, Sir Gilbert 106, 148
Scouring the White Horse 78
Seive making 67
Seven barrows 79
Shannon 127
Sheep 18, 47, 58-9
Shefford, Great 74
Shillingford 104, 106
Shoe making 66, 64, 76
Silk making 66, 94
Southampton 64
South Oxfordshire Hunt 100
Sparsholt 10, 15, 29, 47, 87
Stanford-in-the-Vale 14, 43, 49, 100
Steventon 56, 105, 119
Strawberries 29
Street, G. E. 134
Stripping the willow 31
Stroud 64
Sutton Courtenay 18, 28, 35, 47, 68, 95, 111
Swindon 109, 111, 127, 149
Swinford bridge 106
Symonds, Rev Robert 24, 99